W9-ASR-039

Quest for the Necessary

W. H. AUDEN AND THE DILEMMA OF DIVIDED CONSCIOUSNESS

Quest for the Necessary

W. H. AUDEN AND THE DILEMMA
OF DIVIDED CONSCIOUSNESS

By Herbert Greenberg

HARVARD UNIVERSITY PRESS
Cambridge, Massachusetts
1968

Distributed in Great Britain by Oxford University Press, London
Library of Congress Catalog Card Number 68-54019
Printed in the United States of America

Prefatory Note

AUDEN is a poet whose oeuvre resembles a landscape, a countryside famous but largely unexplored. A master of idiomatic language, a writer who is always attentive to the need of words to be given the chance to *distinguish* themselves, and an inventor of wonderful emblematic imagery which is at once hard and opaque and as illuminating as symptoms brilliantly diagnosed by a master physician, Auden is ultimately lucid and rational; but the surface of his work can be baffling.

The truth of Auden's poetry rests partly in the fact that, however dazzling the effects, it offers at every point a paraphrasable prose meaning, and it can always be traced back to the systems of ideas from which, in its different stages, it derives. No doubt there are readers for whom this poetry of imagination which is always material for intellectual understanding is explicit. But there are many other readers—among whom I count myself—who often feel in reading Auden that they need a guide. And from what I am saying I hope it is clear that I mean they can legitimately claim one, so long as he is a good guide. Herbert Greenberg leads one on from poem to poem through the stages of Auden's development intelligently and sympathetically. His assertion that the central subject of Auden's poetry is the situation of the divided self, and that although his beliefs and philosophy have changed he has always been remarkably consistent in using ideas to analyze that situation, is surely true. This is a lucid and helpful book.

STEPHEN SPENDER

Acknowledgments

LIKE any writer on an established subject, I am much indebted to those who have preceded me: to Richard Hoggart and his early study, *Auden, An Introductory Essay* (London: Chatto & Windus, 1951); to Monroe Spears, particularly with regard to the helpful essays preceding his *The Poetry of W. H. Auden: The Disenchanted Island* (New York: Oxford University Press, 1963); to many others who have published on Auden and whose notions I have assimilated beyond recall. I must mention, too, an unpublished doctoral dissertation which first initiated me to the mysteries of the early work, Justin M. Replogle's "The Auden Group: The 1930's Poetry of W. H. Auden, C. Day Lewis, and Stephen Spender" (University of Wisconsin, 1956).

I am grateful to my colleagues in the Department of English at Michigan State University for two Research Professorships enabling me to pursue my work and to the Humanities Research Center and the All-University Research Fund of Michigan State University for funds to cover the cost of preparing the manuscript for publication.

A debt of a more personal sort I owe to Professor Paul Wiley for many helpful suggestions relating to an earlier version of this study. Miss Janet Yacht did me a timely favor when materials I wished to consult were not at hand. Finally, I must acknowledge my gratitude to Stephen Spender; his kind introductory note is only one example of the generous encouragement I have had from him.

Grateful acknowledgment is extended to Random House, Inc. for the use of copyright material from the works of W. H.

Auden, copyright 1930-©1964. Permission has been granted by Faber and Faber Ltd. to reprint quotations from the works of W. H. Auden to which they hold copyright. Permission to reprint passages from *The Dance of Death,* from *Poems* by W. H. Auden (copyright 1934 by The Modern Library, Inc.), and from *Letters from Iceland* by W. H. Auden and Louis MacNeice (copyright 1937 by W. H. Auden and Louis MacNeice, copyright 1965 by W. H. Auden) has been granted by Curtis Brown, Ltd.

I am greatly obliged to W. H. Auden for authorization to quote from his works.

H. G.

Contents

Quest for the Necessary

W. H. AUDEN AND THE DILEMMA

OF DIVIDED CONSCIOUSNESS

CHAPTER I

Introduction: At the Core

To set in order—that's the task
Both Eros and Apollo ask . . .
—"New Year Letter"

Coming out of me living is always thinking,
Thinking changing and changing living . . .
—"Easter 1929"

THIS book is a study of Auden's poetry as it comes to a focus around the idea of divided consciousness. Its aim is to supply a "reading" of Auden's work through an analysis of the intellectual development informing his inquiry into contemporary circumstances and the underlying human condition. It will hardly be denied that Auden is a poet deeply committed to an intellectual perspective and with a strong systematizing bent, yet the coherence of his intellectual development has often been doubted, and, not surprisingly, the task of elucidating his poems within the framework of this development has been shirked. Without implying that poetry may be reduced to ideas or to the promulgation of an outlook, I would suggest that an adequate appreciation of Auden requires a placing of his work within the context of the governing ideas relevant to its understanding. I do not mean to indicate by this a concern on my part with the history of ideas, nor am I greatly interested, though regardful of influences too important to be ignored, in intellectual sources and contemporary movements of thought. Divided consciousness, I would suggest, is more than a controlling idea in Auden's thought; it is the principal subject matter of his poetry, and it provides the conceptual foundation for his way of looking at things. My effort in the following pages is to offer an interpretation of Auden's work grounded in those preoccupations which seem to me to give coherence to his achievement.

Two objectives are served by this method. Though Auden has remained committed to his religious position for over twenty-five years now, and critics are no longer, as was once the case, apt to resent his conversion or prior shifts in position, there is still a wary reluctance to concede that he has always been an intellectually responsible observer of human affairs, bringing to his task sustained insights. By drawing attention to his interest in divided consciousness, I would hope to correct this impression. Once it is clear that Auden has been concerned with a single issue from the start, the continuity underlying his intellectual development is apparent. My second aim is not a wholly different matter. There has always been something of the *enfant terrible* in Auden, and today, when his work is characterized by what might be called a sly sincerity, this description is as true as ever; but Auden is not only a lively and alert observer, and a provocative analyst; he is also—and perhaps this is more evident today than ever before—a very wise man. I hope to lend weight to John Blair's suggestion that he is in "the great tradition of moral and philosophic poets whose vision probes the nature of human nature."[1]

This having been said, it becomes necessary to acknowledge the challenge posed by the late Randall Jarrell, who, in 1945, in an article entitled "From Freud to Paul: The Stages of Auden's Ideology,"[2] argued that Auden's views were undermined by the presence of obvious psychological determinants. This is a hostile essay, presumably because Jarrell believed that in becoming a Christian Auden had turned his back on the need for social and political action. Monroe Spears reports that he was denied permission to reprint this essay in the Auden volume of the Twentieth

[1] *The Poetic Art of W. H. Auden* (Princeton: Princeton University Press, 1965), p. 189.

[2] *Partisan Review,* XII (Fall 1945), pp. 437-57.

Century Views series,[3] and one infers from this a regret on the author's part for offenses of tone and general immoderateness. It is unfortunate that the essay is not widely available, for many of Jarrell's observations are perceptive, as is his central contention that "A complex of ideas, emotions and unconscious attitudes about anxiety, guilt and isolation" have constituted the "permanent causal core" of Auden's thinking. Concerning those changes of belief taking place in the 1930's and culminating in Auden's conversion, Jarrell offered the following interpretation:

> After observing in Auden this permanent anxiety, guilt, and isolation, adhered to with unchanging firmness in every stage of his development, justified for different reasons in every stage, we cannot fail to see that these "reasons" are reinforcing rationalizations of the related attitudes which, not even rationally considered —much less understood—have been for Auden a core impervious to any change.

The main observation underlying this charge, the insistence that anxiety, guilt, and isolation, are persistent Auden themes, is certainly valid, although Jarrell offers little evidence for thinking that these factors demand a Freudian explanation; we may be forgiven the doubt that Auden's attitudes signify nothing more than a conflict with authority. In any case, Auden's views cannot be nullified simply by calling them "rationalizations," particularly when the "rational" understanding felt to be required refers to a Freudian view of things. Not only has Auden been keenly aware of Freud and, in this sense, "rationally considered," not just his own, but his generation's predicament, he was a conspicuous

[3] *Auden: A Collection of Critical Essays* (Englewood Cliffs, N.J.: Prentice-Hall, 1964), p. 4. Spears' view (p. 3) of Auden's development, in its general drift although not in details, agrees with my own: "As one looks back from the perspective of 1964, it is clear that the changes were confined to one brief period in the late Thirties, that they were all in the same direction, and that, once the fundamental commitment to Christianity had been fully made, the only changes were mere shifts of emphasis."

champion of Freudianism, who rejected the Freudian view as inadequate only after a considerable period of advocacy. One recalls at this point Nathan A. Scott's suggestion that much of the critical irritation encountered by Auden may be traced to a commitment to Christianity reached "only after every alternative to the Christian faith [had] been faced and evaluated."[4]

But not only those with a position to defend have found Auden's fluctuations in outlook disturbing. The view that he is a "chameleon poet," with a mind prone to excess, has been suggested by a friend, C. Day Lewis, who has remarked that the dogmas of one year are, with Auden, likely to be the heresies of the next.[5] Again, there is justice in the charge, for Auden has not been apologetic in publicly revising his views or particularly ingenuous about the learning process implicit in his development. But his poetry is the record of such a process, and it would be a mistake to allow tones occasionally pontifical to obscure this fact or the extent to which he has endeavored, and has managed, to see life steadily and with respect for the whole.

Anxiety, guilt, and isolation are at the core of his effort, and whether one's personal explanation of the significance of these factors in human experience be ultimately Freudian or existential, Auden has been more than aware that they are elements relevant to his work; he has carefully indicated their relevance. I am not suggesting that he is an existential poet, writing from the depths of subjective dread, or even that his thought has always found expression in existential categories. As Stephen Spender has observed, Auden has endeavored to maintain a perspective transcending that of individual experience, his concern being "to shift the center of his dogmatic ways of regarding experience from himself to some objective authority, so that he himself becomes a part

[4] "The Poetry of Auden," *Chicago Review,* XXII (Winter 1959), p. 54.

[5] *The Buried Day* (London: Chatto & Windus, 1960), p. 25.

of what is judged."[6] This concern, however, may be taken as a response to the human situation existentially conceived, for this foundation serves as a point of departure for his inquiry into complex issues. In his capacity as a critic of capitalism and its reenforcing morality, his focus is not on abstract injustice or economic inequity but on impoverished experience, the sorry dilemma of individuals whose natural impulses are frustrated by internalized social restrictions. Thus, although he has not always treated his themes in existentialist terms, his judgments on matters of general consequence, such as the organization of society or the problem of belief, have been centered around freedom and limitation as the principal experiences of human life. And the role of anxiety in his work may be understood from this point of view, for he points out that it is the point of view not only of a philosopher such as Kierkegaard but of "what is most valuable" in the contribution of earlier mentors, Marx and Freud:

> From this point of view, the basic human problem is man's anxiety in time; e.g., his present anxiety over himself in relation to his past and his parents (Freud), his present anxiety over himself in relation to his future and his neighbors (Marx), his present anxiety over himself in relation to eternity and God (Kierkegaard).[7]

Auden's problem has always been, then, the problem of our anxiety in connection with those factors shaping our relationship to ourselves, and, phrased another way, it has been characterized as the ultimate pressing question of our time: "Where do we, where shall we, where can we derive our moral sanctions—from a failing tradition or from the wild free impulses of our racial infancy, from the Ego or the Id?"[8] Auden has considered the prob-

[6] "W. H. Auden and His Poetry," *Atlantic Monthly,* CXCII (July 1953), p. 75.

[7] "A Preface to Kierkegaard," *New Republic,* CX (May 1944), p. 683.

[8] Diana Trilling, "Norman Mailer," *Encounter,* XIX (Nov. 1962), p. 53.

lem in terms bearing a close resemblance to these, for our anxiety arises from divided consciousness, a condition defined in his assertion that "Man's being is a copulative relation between a subject ego and a predicate self." As agent of mental awareness and volition, the "ego" is the unique consciousness seeming to each individual wholly free and coincident with his experience of personal being, while the "self" is that part of himself which seems separable from himself and, as object of the ego's attention, seems "given, already there in the world, finite, derived, along with, related and comparable to other beings."[9] This basic distinction may be regarded from endless perspectives: the ego is the "I" part of ourselves, the self the "me"; as the beholder of possibility and relationship, the ego may be identified with "imagination," but it is equally the agent of "reason"; the self, on the other hand, is the source of instinct, the emotions, and of unconscious needs; crudely conceived, the ego is mind, the self body. Furthermore, project this subjective division into the frame of reference of the objective multitudinous world, and it appears as that between "history" and "nature," realms in which we confront, respectively, those factors weaving a complex thematic pattern in the texture of Auden's work—freedom and necessity.

Though at different times certain formulations of the distinction between ego and self are more applicable to an understanding of Auden than others, all imply a constant view of the human condition. Conceive the opposition as narrowly as that, say, between "will" and "desire," or so broadly as to encompass conscious mind with all its cultural predispositions on the one hand and, on the other, vital energy, the Id, or the Unconscious; the unvarying problem is that the ego stands isolated in its experience of freedom, a prey to the anxiety of relating the individual to the world and of seeking for this purpose a viable knowledge of and relationship

[9] *The Enchafèd Flood* (New York: Random House, 1959; London: Faber and Faber, 1951); my quotations are from the British edition; see p. 102.

with the self. Whatever the indebtedness of Auden's thought, whether to the psychology of Homer Lane or D. H. Lawrence, or to Marx, or to the Christian existentialism of Kierkegaard or Reinhold Niebuhr, what he is primarily doing is seeking an answer to the fundamental question of how ego and self shall inter-relate; his debt to these authors is a response to the analysis they offer of this problem; his underlying interest is in the principle envisioned as guiding this relationship towards the end of individual fulfillment.

The pursuit of such a principle is evident in a Quest for what he has variously referred to as the Necessary, the Unconditional, or the Logos. Stephen Spender is right, however, when he suggests that the direction of Auden's poetry has been "towards the defining of the concept of love,"[10] for the two processes are identical. If Auden has consistently addressed himself to the question "How shall we live?" his conviction that love is the basic energy of life has provided that the question mean, essentially, "How shall we love?" And love has always implied for him what the title of a a well-known poem, "Law Like Love," suggests: namely "law," in the sense of "natural law," but also in the broader sense of "that which is required of us." The conception derives from Dante, whose influence has been seminal and long-lasting, for Dante provides the organizing framework by means of which the problem of ego and self is construed as involving a quality of love. Auden has acknowledged his indebtedness by referring at least eight times to the following passage from the seventeenth canto of the *Purgatory*:[11]

[10] "W. H. Auden and his Poetry," p. 78.

[11] The references are as follows: *The Orators,* in *Poems* (New York: Random House, 1934), p. 94; "The Group Movement and the Middle Classes," in *Oxford and the Groups,* ed. R. H. S. Crossman (Oxford: Basil Blackwell, 1934), p. 96; "The Good Life," in *Christianity and the Social Revolution,* ed. John Lewis (London: Victor Gollancz, 1935), p. 36; "Psychology and Art To-Day," in *The Arts To-Day,* ed. Geoffrey Grigson (London: John Lane, The Bodley Head, 1935), p. 13; "What is Culture?"

> "Nor Creator, nor creature, my son, was ever without
> love, either natural or rational; and this thou
> knowest.
> The natural is always without error; but the other
> may err through an evil object, or through too little
> or too much vigour . . .
> ". . . Hence thou may'st understand that love must be the
> seed of every virtue in you, and of every deed that
> deserves punishment."

Two things must be noted here: first, the insistence that living properly is a matter of appropriately loving, of properly actualizing the basic energies attendant upon the gift of life; second, the distinction between these energies as, on the one hand, inseparable from life and the expression of selfhood, and, on the other, controlled by the exercise of the ego's freedom. Dante's distinction between *Amor Naturale* and *Amor Rationalis* formulates the problem of divided consciousness, and by associating Dante's natural love with the Freudian "Eros," with what the psychologist Georg Groddeck called the "It" and Blake (and apparently Homer Lane also) called "Desire," with Jung's and D. H. Lawrence's "Unconscious," and also, in a sense, with God, Auden has been able to bring to bear on this matter the insights of a wide range of modern thought. Love Natural is the basic stuff of life, and Auden's problem has been to discover its demands upon us and particularly upon the ego: each revision in his thinking may be regarded as a renewed effort to answer the question of how and by what authority love is to fulfill itself in a divided creature.

In light of this observation, and though it is possible, as I shall point out, to describe Auden's development as a progression through the Kierkegaardian categories of the Aesthetic, the Ethi-

---

Nation, CLI (July 1940), p. 18; "Eros and Agape," *Nation,* CLII (June 1941), p. 757; "Notes," *New Year Letter* (London: Faber and Faber, 1941); p. 143; "Balaam and His Ass," *The Dyer's Hand* (New York: Random House, 1962), p. 130.

cal, and the Religious, there is much to recommend the common view which sees him as first under the influence of a psychological perspective (the early thirties), then as drawn, although without abandoning this perspective, towards Marxism (the mid-thirties) and, after a time, with the erosion of the Marxist view of historical necessity, towards what might be called humanism or liberal humanitarianism (the late thirties), and, finally, around 1940, to Christianity; for each of these periods reveals a distinctive conception of Love, which is to say, of the Necessary, embodied in a different conception of the relationship to be maintained between ego and self.

From the premise that the basic energy of the universe is love, certain propositions follow. They are expressed in the first two of the following statements of belief recorded in 1949:

(a) All created existence is a good.
(b) Evil is a negative perversion of created good.
(c) Man has free will to choose between good and evil.
(d) But all men are sinners with a perverted will.[12]

If statements (a) and (b) have always been for Auden absolute presuppositions, (c) and (d) represent critical developments in his thinking. The notion that all men are sinners with a perverted will reflects his acceptance of Christianity, and is, in fact, an observation of major relevance in causing this acceptance; while the doctrine of free will, though never denied by him, would have proven acceptable at some stages only with serious reservations which, when modified, mark turning points in his career.

The problem of love in relation to the efficacy of the will in dealing with evil is, in fact, insofar as any one factor may be singled out in this connection, the issue ultimately prompting each major change in Auden's views. It is possible here to trace his thinking only in bald outline, with elaboration to follow in suc-

[12] "The Question of the Pound Award," *Partisan Review,* XVI (May 1949), p. 513.

ceeding chapters; but we may note that in the early work, freedom, regarded as the rational exercise of the will, has little import in his scheme of values. The early work takes its clue from Lawrence's contention that man has a mind and his problem is that he can't get used to the fact; its assault is directed against the ideas and narrow ideals created by mind and intervening between vital unconscious desires and their fulfillment. "Love" at this point means the gratification of energies, a "Necessary" because the stifling of energies leads to disease. England is "this country of ours where nobody is well," and for Auden "cure" means giving vent to desire and spontaneity of impulse, to a freedom, not *of* the will, but *from* it and its false consciousness, so as to release the more vital promptings of the unconscious. The trouble is that cure is more easily envisioned than effected, that in a sick society even unconscious impulses are diseased and display the effects of repression. It is when Auden realizes this that freedom in the other sense of consciousness of choice becomes meaningful to him. With this recognition, he becomes hospitable to Marxism and its conviction that social change must precede the regeneration of the individual. Much as Marx sees in control of the state a means to achieve its ultimate withering away, Auden discovers that health will be genuinely accessible only when the ill, with an understanding of their illness, commit themselves, not to personal liberation, but to the social task of abolishing the conditions which make personal liberation generally unattainable.

Although the awareness that illness, as neurotic self-interest or as a fear of change, may corrupt the understanding just as effectively as it perverts the will to be well, makes for a wary assessment of the likelihood of effective social action, Auden's respectful reevaluation of freedom of the will is strengthened by historical circumstance. With the emergence of fascism as a threat to individual liberty, his interim commitment to the utility of the will is established on a new foundation. Freedom, he comes to see, is the capacity separating man from the beasts, it is the defining characteristic of the species. If man's freedom accounts for the fact that, unlike the beasts, he goes wrong, this is a price well-paid for his capacity to be a creative agent in his own evolution. For freedom means "consciousness of necessity," a developing knowledge not only of the world but of the self; it is indispensable, Auden decides, to human fulfillment, which requires an interplay between freedom and necessity, a "wrestling" bout between the self as given and the ego as shaper of possibility. Love for Auden now means, not merely vitality, or, as times require, social commitment to the goal of vitality; it means the *humanizing* of vitality. Love is the principle we define in acknowledging our interdependence and in enriching the sense of what it means to be human.

It should be understood that conversion does not essentially alter this view of things. Far from repudiating the need for social and political action, Auden as a Christian has found in his faith a foundation for his commitment to the "Just City," and though he often chooses to appear today as the champion of an unpolitical "Arcadia," this is a guise adopted by craft and reflecting a concern more actue than ever with the character of the "Truly Human" and with the values of the City. But his hopes are no longer informed by a belief in knowledge as our ultimate salvation. He has discovered that to know the good is not necessarily to will it, and in this fact there stands revealed for him our dependence upon God. For Christianity represents for Auden a coming to terms with the problem of evil as insoluble by human effort alone. If his development has been an endeavor to define the meaning of love, it has also, necessarily, been an effort to understand the obstacles frustrating love and testing the validity of his conclusions. During his secular period, when he had sought to discover the meaning of love from an analysis of human nature, this effort had necessitated accounting for evil as a separable phenomenon, as arising from illness or from impaired or inadequate knowledge, factors not obviously inherent in us and therefore presumably removable. The war put an end to the effort. It convinced him that human nature was not the foundation for humanistic principles, that it was only by reference to an authority outside the self that these principles could be regarded as unconditional. Accepting the Christian conception of love as *agape*, a goal to which we are urged by divine commandment, Auden also accepts the myth of the Fall, not as referring to the acquisition of self-consciousness—the import he had previously acknowledged—but as revealing our innate self-love and need of Grace. Located in an inherent perversion of will, evil is finally accepted into the system which accounts for it.

The major danger in a study of a poet primarily concerned with the ideas shaping his work and dividing it into "periods" is that it will overschematize and oversimplify, that it will distort the individual poem in an effort to enforce its representative import. E. M. Forster once observed that it was difficult to be both impressive and truthful, and I have many times been reminded of this in attempting to describe a pertinence in Auden not always clearly brought to the surface of particular poems or in giving to certain details in a poem an emphasis that context, quite improperly from my point of view, had neglected to establish. In defense of an approach which makes experiences such as these unavoidable to a certain extent, I offer two observations. The first is that there seems to me a value in understanding Auden's intellectual development even apart from its relevance to his poetry. Auden has been a sensitive interpreter of his time, and as one among many writers preoccupied with the problem of divided consciousness his efforts illuminate, not only his time, but major movements in twentieth-century thought. Second, and more important, although ideas are not the substance of Auden's poetry, I would argue that the conceptualizing process plays a role in his work, and a poetic role, much more important than contemporary criticism would lead us to expect. Today, we tend to assess richness in a poem according to the clarity or to the intensity of its response to the implications of felt experience; but this is a view not readily applicable to a poet inclined to be directly concerned with the general import of things, rather than with their evocativeness or their personal impact. Monroe K. Spears has done valuable service recently by drawing attention to the importance of song in Auden, a topic concerning which the following pages will have little to contribute; but it seems to me that Auden's distinction lies not so much in his lyrical versatility, considerable though this is, as in the vividness of his intelligence, that it is as an earnest or, more recently, as an artful observer of complex relationships that he most valuably commands our attention. Thus, although I could wish my study many things that it is not, and particularly regret that it was impossible to combine with a method geared primarily to the exposition of meaning a fuller treatment of Auden's art, and of the relationship between outlook and poetic technique, I am content that my approach be judged by the light it sheds. Because Auden's poetry is anchored in an examination of human existence, the problems with which he has wrestled intellectually are recurrent themes in his art, the categories shaping his inquiry function as sources of imagery, and the ideas that have controlled his thought also inform his poetic strategies.

CHAPTER II

The Thwarted Self

PAID ON BOTH SIDES—POEMS—THE ORATORS

For daily under the disguise of immediate day-dream
Or nightly in direct vision the man is nourished,
Fed through the essential artery of memory
Out of the earth the mother of all life . . .

—*Poems* (1930)

There is a wound and who shall staunch it up?
Deepening daily, discharging all the time
Power from love.

—Uncollected poem[1]

CHANGE, as a separation from the fixed and unproductive, as a necessity of growth and a law of temporal life, is an essential element in Auden's way of looking at things. Unlike a poet such as Yeats, whose proclivities oscillate between being and becoming, so that his development is a tug of war between time and eternity, Auden stands centered in the temporal process. To Yeats, history is cyclical, civilization a turning of the gyres; to Auden, cyclical recurrence is a feature of nature, and history means linear movement, a thrust into novelty made possible by our freedom. It was not always this way. To Auden too at one time, at the time of the early poetry we are about to examine, history seemed merely nature expressing itself through human societies, or struggling to express itself, and human choice a "necessary error"; and later he too would prove susceptible to the thirst for being, the experience of the "garden" in a moment out of time. But always his attention has

[1] See the second of "Five Poems," *New Verse* (Oct. 1933), p. 15.

remained anchored in the process of living itself, the obligation to confront the exigencies of the temporal moment. The question, "How shall we live? How shall we love?" has always been for Auden a very practical one, and he has sought an answer that would satisfy his awareness that change and renewal must be a law of life.

Despite the perplexing features of the early work, change is clearly the issue focussing Auden's interests, a basis for petition and appeal: ". . . look shining at/ New styles of architecture, a change of heart," for the scornful denunciation of "Holders of one position, wrong for years," for ominous notes of warning: "It is time for the destruction of error." But change is also a prospect arousing anxieties and a sense of futility: we encounter repeatedly in the early poetry revolutionaries who have failed in their task or seem doomed to failure, and enlightened individuals who remain bound by their fears to inaction. There is a sense of coming upheaval anticipated with impatience, but there is also an awareness of enervating inertia, of ineffectuality at a time of crisis:

> The opening window, closing door,
> Open, close, but not
> To finish or restore . . .
>
> (Poem VI, "Between attention and attention"[2])

[2] Auden's early belief that poems should be untitled makes unavoidable this cumbersome method of citation by reference to first lines; but there is some consolation in the fact that *The Collected Poetry of W. H. Auden* (New York: Random House, 1945; London: Faber and Faber, 1948) and *Collected Shorter Poems 1930-44* (London: Faber and Faber, 1950) are arranged for the most part alphabetically, by first lines. However, these volumes have now been superseded by *Collected Shorter Poems 1927-57* (New York: Random House, 1967; London: Faber and Faber, 1966). Though I occasionally use a title devised for the 1945 *Collected Poetry,* readers are warned that the text of the poem may differ from the original to which I am referring. Unless otherwise mentioned, my quotations in this chapter are from the 1934 *Poems* (New York: Random House). Like the original *Poems* (London: Faber and Faber, 1930), this useful edition contains "Paid on Both Sides," but it also reprints *The Orators* (1932) and

Peace in this setting, when achieved, is a momentary insulation against threatening forces. Not only is a time of reckoning at hand, there are also enemies to be guarded against, an anonymous "They" that has "severed all the wires," that appears in cunning disguises and seems allied, not to change, but to death. The "We's" who oppose play a curiously ambiguous role: they participate in the sense of cool and knowing detachment that characterizes the poet's voice, but they are often just those partisans of the future who seem unequal to its burdens, the failed revolutionaries and timid farers.

Original readers of *Poems* (1930) and *The Orators* (1932) would have had a stronger sense of the general social significance of the intentness upon crisis and change than do those readers who come to these works today without an experience of the early thirties or with, at best, a dim recollection of the social anxiety of the time—the widespread feeling that things could not go on much longer as they had, that civilization was approaching catastrophe. Still, it is clear that even early readers found it no easy task to make headway with the poems. Dramatic representations for the most part, and mainly untitled, these poems often seem to deliberately withhold from the reader any indication of authorial attitude or intent. A surface of laconic statement, produced by ellipsis and an irregular syntax, operates to obscure the literal sense of things, intensifying the problem of establishing the precise context of reference within which circumstances occur or the background of assumption against which they have meaning. Repeated glimpses of a landscape blighted by unused rail lines and rotting machinery, "silted harbours, derelict works," testify to a concern

---

The Dance of Death (1933), both first published in London by Faber and Faber. In *The Making of the Auden Canon* (Minneapolis: University of Minnesota Press, 1957), Joseph Warren Beach discusses, in an appendix, poems appearing only in the 1930 edition of *Poems* and in subsequent editions, beginning with that of 1933 (London: Faber and Faber), replaced by others. I am mainly concerned with the revised text of *Poems.*

with an industrial society in decay; but mysterious references to spies and to the "frontier," to battles and insurrections waged by unidentified individuals against unnamed opponents under circumstances uncertain, to enigmatic love relationships and private persons (Ciddy, Fronny, Captain Ferguson)—all of these collaborate with Auden's announced preference for a posture of clinical detachment to render troublesome the precise relationship of the poems to social realities.

Auden has said that wherever there is a creative gift there is also a "guilty secret" and that, as a consequence, the first productions of young poets are usually a "catharsis of resentment."[3] This statement would seem to support some of Randall Jarrell's contentions regarding the early work, such as the suggestion that the doomed heroes who appear so regularly are really a projection of Auden's own feelings of guilt and have little to do with ideology. But readers of a work such as Christopher Isherwood's *Lions and Shadows* will recognize that Auden's catharsis was one shared with contemporaries, that the interest in spies and such types as the neurotic hero and his opposite, the "truly strong man," and the notion of a war between the younger generation and their oppressors, reflect a fund of schoolboy fantasy shared with such friends as Stephen Spender, Cecil Day Lewis, Edward Upward, and Isherwood himself, who had constructed their rebellious attitude towards established authority into a private mythology of opposition.[4] In this mythology, as we may judge from Isherwood's no-

[3] "The Rewards of Patience," *Partisan Review,* IX (July-August 1942), p. 337.

[4] What *Lions and Shadows* reveals less conclusively is the extent to which the poems may refer to particular events of a private character. If we are on the alert, we are continually teased by resemblances that might or might not be pertinent—that between Isherwood's description of his invalid role and "Letter to a Wound," or Ode III of *The Orators* ("What siren zooming"), dedicated to Edward Upward, and Upward's (Chalmers') characterization of his and Isherwood's initiation to Cambridge as an "arrival at the country of the dead."

tion of the "Test," the friends self-consciously projected and examined their feelings of self-doubt. The process by which resentment and insecurity are analyzed and understood is one continually going on in Auden's work and in which the element of directed inquiry (with the theoretical underpinnings it implies) is present from the first.

We may take as a starting point a passage from "Paid on Both Sides," spoken by a figure called the "Man-Woman," a personification of Eros:

> Because I'm come it does not mean to hold
> An anniversary, think illness healed,
> As to renew the lease, consider costs
> Of derelict ironworks on deserted coasts.
> Love was not love for you but episodes,
> Traffic in memoirs, views from different sides;
> . . . .
> I lay with you; you made that an excuse
> For playing with yourself, but homesick because
> Your mother told you that's what flowers did,
> And thought you lived since you were bored, not dead,
> And could not stop. So I was cold to make
> No difference, but you were quickly meek
> Altered for safety. I tried then to demand
> Proud habits, protestations called you mind
> To show you it was extra, but instead
> You overworked yourself, misunderstood,
> Adored me for the chance. Lastly I tried
> To teach you acting, but always you had nerves
> To fear performances as some fear knives.

The sense of this is not easy and perhaps not fully coherent, but the main counts of the indictment are clear. This is a society wedded to illness by the force of its own fears, incapable of any but an immature sexuality, unspontaneous, eager to sidetrack its energies—

unable to establish a vital relationship with Eros. Against this background, one can make sense of the early work. Authentic life has always been the goal of Auden's quest, and under this heading, shaping the theme of the old life versus the new, the features of the early work gain meaning: it is the quest for the new life that spurs the revolutionaries to action and the secret agents to their duties; those denounced as the "enemy" are representatives of the old and its willing perpetrators; it is the decadence of this life that is objectified in landscape, and freedom from its oppressive hold that lies across the frontier. The central metaphor vindicating new allegiances is that of disease: the old life is diseased, the new life represents health. The old life is arraigned because it lacks the power to cure itself: Health demands change and growth, it demands, precisely, *evolution*; and the old order has grown rigid.

Owing to the psychological theories influencing Auden, the disease metaphor has a literal basis. Those "once healers in our native land," D. H. Lawrence, William Blake, and Homer Lane, had perhaps the most immediate impact, but others, like Freud, Jung, Gerald Heard, and the German psychologist Georg Groddeck, also played their role. What unites these writers is a common respect for the vital energies of the unconscious, a recognition that individuals and whole societies may come to grief when they rigorously suppress these energies, call them "libido," "instinct," or simply the "unconscious." Homer Lane apparently called them "Desire," and important in his teachings—at least as Auden received them from a disciple, John Layard, during a trip to Germany in 1928-29—is a vigorous identification, allying him in particular with Lawrence, of the ego faculties of reason and conscious direction as the principal source of human distress. Here for example, is Lawrence:

> It is the impulse we have to live by, not the ideals or the idea . . . Mental consciousness is a purely individual affair. Some men are

> born to be highly and delicately conscious. But for the vast majority, much mental consciousness is simply a catastrophe, a blight. It just stops their living.[5]

As they appear in Edward Upward's *Journey to the Border*,[6] Lane's views are even more sweeping. "Conflict" is a product of reason, we are told, whereas "Unrepressed Desire is always gay and friendly"; from our failure to obey it come not only sickness but "poverty and war and slavery and all the social evils of our time":

> To the sufferer . . . Conscious Control must always appear noble and right, because the whole natural system has been inverted for him in childhood. He cannot regard Desire otherwise than as something ignoble and wrong. Therefore his salvation lies in being "unreasonable," in rejecting what is "right," and doing what is "wrong."

Presumably, Freud's divergence from this view accounts for his unexpected appearance among "Those who have betrayed us" in Poem XXII ("Get there if you can").

According to Lane, diseases result from "disobedience to the inner law of our own nature" and are warnings to the soul, attempts by the unconscious to effect a cure. While this belief is paralleled in Auden's other mentors, including Lawrence ("There is nothing

[5] *Fantasia of the Unconscious,* in *Psychoanalysis and the Unconscious, Fantasia of the Unconscious* (New York: Viking Press, 1962), pp. 105-06.

[6] I attribute to Lane the views voiced by Gregory Mavors on no authority other than Isherwood's report (in *Lions and Shadows*) that he forwarded Lane's views to Upward, and because of the resemblance between what Mavors is made to say and Isherwood's summary, which has been quoted often enough. The attribution may not be fair to Lane, but since Lane wrote very little and Auden seems to have known nothing of his work firsthand, what is important here is only the question of what Auden and his friends took to be the Lane point of view. This seems clearly expressed in the passages from *Journey to the Border* (London: Hogarth Press, 1938), p. 140.

inside us, we stare endlessly at the outside. So our eyes begin to fail; to retaliate on us. We go shortsighted, almost in self-protection."),[7] again Lane seems to have preached the doctrine with a flamboyance all his own:

> From childhood up, we are taught that our natural desires are evil, that we must control them, deny them room to grow. But they will not be denied. Twisted, clogged with moralizings, driven back from all normal avenues of development, they nevertheless find a way of asserting themselves, appear in disguise, take on unexpected and abnormal forms—malaria, murder, neurosis . . .

Auden melodramatically echoes this view in an uncollected poem which claims that if you refuse life freedom, "You'll find a cancer in your breast/ Or a burglar in your flat."[8]

All of these writers seem to have composed a prophetic tradition for Auden and, seeking the strength of a concurrence of authorities, he often links them together. He notes that the teachings of Lane illuminate the origin of the cardinal errors identified by Blake, which he quotes from *The Marriage of Heaven and Hell*—a work which he claims contains the whole of Freud's teachings—as follows:

> (1)That Man has two real existing principles—a Body and a Soul.
>
> (2) That Energy called evil is alone from the Body; and that Reason, called good, is alone from the Soul.

Underlying and organizing these influences is Dante's conception of *Amor Naturale*, which, as "the basic will to self-actualization without which no creature could exist," is innocent of error, and *Amor Rationalis*, which may err in the measure of its devotion or when devoted to a wrong object. On two occasions, Auden ex-

[7] *Fantasia of the Unconscious,* p. 102.

[8] "Cautionary Rhymes," *Adelphi, III* (Dec. 1931), p. 181.

pressly identifies Love Natural with the Freudian "Eros," while the theories of Lane may owe a direct debt to Dante: "Man does not choose to love. He *must* love," Lane wrote:

> If he hates, his behavior is untrue to himself, to mankind and to the universe, but the energy is still love, for his act of hatred is love perverted.[9]

To be healthy, then, means to follow nature, to restore the authority of the unconscious so as to heal the breach between the reflective ego and the impulsive self. Self-fulfillment for Auden is always a resolution of this duality, issuing in love; but love as he saw it at this time means mainly a satisfying of impulses: the problem is to overthrow the rule of "reason," repressive morality, and false idealism, the malaise of self-consciousness which, internalizing the authority of social prohibition, gets between the individual and his needs and promotes anxiety, guilt, and illness. The same year *Poems* was published, Auden declares that the dualistic notion of a "higher" and "lower" self is the cause of disease, crime, and war: "That which desires life to itself, be it individual, habit, or reason, casts itself like lucifer [sic], out of heaven." But he is fond of pointing out that intellectual curiosity is neurotic, that man only thinks when he is prevented from feeling or acting as he might desire; "duality" seems a bias in only one direction and "heaven" very like the immediacy of undivided consciousness. Two 1935 articles on psychology[10] suggest this view with especial

[9] *Talks to Parents and Teachers* (New York: Hermitage Press, 1949), p. 196. For Auden on Blake and Lane, see "To Unravel Happiness," *Listener,* XII (Nov. 28, 1934), suppl., p. xi; on Blake and Freud: "Psychology and Art To-Day," in *The Arts To-Day,* ed. Geoffrey Grigson (London: John Lane, The Bodley Head, 1935), p. 12; on Freud and Dante: the essay just cited, p. 13, and also "The Good Life," in *Christianity and the Social Revolution,* ed. John Lewis (London: Victor Gollancz, 1935), p. 36. For the definition of Love Natural, see "Eros and Agape," *Nation,* CLII (June 1941), p. 757.

[10] "The Good Life" and "Psychology and Art To-Day." For the comment on duality, see rev. of George Binney Dibblee, *Instinct and Intuition, Criterion,* IX (April 1930), p. 569.

clarity, though written at a time when Auden was changing his mind about its implications. He suggests that "Perfect satisfaction" would consist of "complete unconsciousness," and that the myth of a Golden Age or Garden of Eden is confirmed by contemporary anthropology. This myth and that of the Fall are inevitable to the symbolism of divided consciousness and he will return to both from fresh perspectives. But at this time he interprets the Fall, as does Lawrence, as referring to the introduction of self-consciousness into the primal state: "all that we recognize as evil or sin is its consequence." In the writings of Groddeck,[11] whose key conception is that ailments are psychically caused and may be interpreted, like all other human activities, as symbolic manifestations of an unconscious, undifferentiated force called the "It," a recurrent notion is that we are "lived" by the It. This idea is not, in Groddeck, the clinically productive insight it was to become when systematized by Freud; but, suggesting that self-determination is illusory, it lent strength to the view that the way to live was to cease interfering with life.

As a result, a constant target of scorn, and of an oblique self-criticism, is something Auden refers to as "self-regard," which means not selfishness, although that is a part of it, but a thwarted relationship to one's own needs, encouraging self-centered or fantasy satisfaction rather than real gratification. The state of health is "self-forgetfulness" or that condition which either Auden or Layard (Isherwood is not sure which) described as being "pure in heart," which entails, among other things, since illness is a product of repression or of guilt, immunity from disease.[12] Our griefs stem

[11] See in particular *The Book of the It* (New York: Vintage Books, 1961).

[12] The following, from *Lions and Shadows* (Norfolk: New Directions, 1947, p. 304), is Isherwood's description of the pure in heart individual:

> He was essentially free and easy, generous with his money and belongings, without worries or inhibitions. He would let you brush your teeth with his toothbrush or write with his fountain-pen. He was a wonderful listener, but he never "sympathized" with your

from "disobedience to the inner law of our own nature," and the state of obedience is one of least conscious control, when man is "Pushed on like grass-blade":

> For daily under the disguise of immediate day-dream
> Or nightly in direct vision the man is nourished,
> Fed through the essential artery of memory
> Out of the earth the mother of all life;
> And all that were living flesh at any time,
> The entire record of change in spirit and structure
> Cry in his veins for air, plead to be born,
> Enriching life, which if he refuse and abort,
> Perishing they poison and he become a cypher
> With codified conduct and a vacant vessel for heart.
> Yes, she is always with him and will sustain him;
> Often he knows it—caught in a storm on fells
> And sheltering with horses behind a dripping wall,
> Or in prolonged interview with another's eyes
> And full length contact he will forget himself
> As passion coming to its climax loses identity
> And consciousness, is one with all flesh.[13]

This passage brings together most of the elements mentioned. Life is nourished by the impulses rising from the unconscious; as "memory," this is the rich inheritance we must bring to expression if existence is to be vital but which exerts a poisoning effect when denied spontaneity; at moments of self-forgetfulness, such as the moment of orgasm, when most "lived" by this power, the individual is truly united to life.

Launched on behalf of a liberation of the instincts, Auden's

---

troubles; and the only advice he ever gave was in the form of parables—stories about other people which you could apply to your own problem, if you liked. He was entirely without fear; therefore he could never catch an infectious disease. And without sexual guilt: therefore he was immune from syphilis. Above all, he was profoundly happy.

[13] Poem II, *Poems* (London: Faber and Faber, 1930).

assault on society is directed against stultifying and inhibiting habits, traditions of control starving the passions, and has little to do with any economic or political abstraction. Despite the link later made, the idea of Eros as an evolving social force has no connection at this time with Marxism. As Stephen Spender tells us, although both of them were made aware in Germany of "two revolutions" developing, it was only after experiencing the unemployment of the early thirties and, gradually, "with the rise of fascism, that we accepted the Marxist analysis of the situation that produced Hitler, unemployment and the threat of war."[14] Poem XXII ("Get there if you can"), perhaps the most direct and polemical of the poems threatening cataclysm, rages like its model, "Locksley Hall Sixty Years After," over an array of indignities, including the schemes of big business and unutilized resources; but these are treated less as wrongs to be corrected than as proof of how individuals have been duped. The healthy would not submit to being victimized, the poem implies; and it calls for a revolution not of protest or reform but of health: "Drop those priggish ways for ever, stop behaving like a stone:/ Throw the bath-chairs right away, and learn to leave ourselves alone."

The new life Auden hopes for is one of freedom from the "rehearsed response" and the "coward's stance," of cure for the "intolerable neural itch." These things are prayed for in Poem XXX, now called "Petition," where the arresting juxtaposition "New styles of architecture, a change of heart," shows them related to social evolution; for health in society means flexibility and adaptability to change. Lawrence insists that the "whole point" about the unconscious is "that it is all the time moving forward, beyond the range of its own fixed laws and habits,"[15] and probably Auden's celebrated concern with the "death wish" is best understood as an inability to adapt to such movement. Occasionally the wish is con-

[14] "It Began at Oxford," *New York Times Book Review,* March 13, 1955, pp. 4-5.

[15] *Psychoanalysis and the Unconscious,* p. 16.

ceived in Freudian terms as distinct from Eros and in opposition to it, but the characteristic conception is that of "Petition," where it is represented as the sin against the Holy Ghost and characterized as "will, its negative inversion." Thus, like "every virtue in you . . . and every deed that deserves punishment," its source is ultimately love; but it is love's means of eliminating those who refuse love development, who have perverted it out of a fear of life into an attachment for the past which, as the rejection of change and growth, is the love of death.

History for Auden, meaning not men and deeds but evolutionary process, the generic achievements of the life force, is the point of view from which the suspect virtues of the establishment are seen through. If T. S. Eliot's assessment of history is "Gerontion," Auden's—early Auden's—is "Since you are going to begin today" (Poem III), which echoes Eliot's poem. Again the speaker is Eros, who "shifted ranges, lived epochs handicapped," "Whose cleverest invention was lately fur"—and who provides, thus, a vantage from which all attainment is revealed as tentative and temporary:

> Think—Romans had a language in their day
> And ordered roads with it, but it had to die . . .

The unforgivable sin against evolution is, in "Gerontion's" words, to think it possible to "reach conclusion." Scrutinized by Eros, upper class manners and form appear not as denouement but as desperate disguise:

> Others have tried it and will try again
> To finish that which they did not begin:
> Their fate must always be the same as yours,
> To suffer the loss they were afraid of, yes,
> Holders of one position, wrong for years.[16]

[16] Cf. Lawrence's foreword to *Women in Love* (New York: Viking Press, 1960, p. viii): "We are now in a period of crisis. Every man who is acutely alive is acutely wrestling with his own soul. The people that can bring forth the new passion, the new idea, this people will en-

The evolutionary outlook is also implemented in broadly satiric terms of the music-hall variety. In Poem IX ("It's no use raising a shout"), the "wish" in the veins is the response of Eros to an environmental impasse of a type met and surmounted in the past. But the speaker is out of touch with the life of inner vitality (the "base" in the spine is Lawrence's "lumbar ganglion") and can only despair ("Here am I, here are you:/ But what does it mean? What are we going to do?"). Unable to face the future, he sees himself at a dead-end in a process proving only the inadequacy of, successively, water, land, and love as fulfilling environments.

Though one can never be certain of having grasped the point of some of these poems, certain motifs offer helpful clues. The past and the present, fathers and sons, are recurrent oppositions, and "family ghosts" (a title late given Poem XX) are continually evoked from albums or from memory to reveal the degeneracy of effete heirs. "Father by son/ Lives on" in the "conquerors" of Poem XXI ("On Sunday walks"), but the wish to preserve old forms of patronage towards dependents and inferiors now enforces "make-believe"; sons performing their daily duties with an appearance of equanimity are in their dreams "pursued by eaters"; what used to be a fear of "fever and bad luck" has become "a scare/ At certain names/ A need for charms." Like Lawrence's, Auden's dissatisfaction with the structure of society has little to do with the privileges and wealth enjoyed by a limited class; the point of the injustice is that those in power no longer possess vital authority, represent an exhausted mode of life. The "gracious greeting" of the "loved one" in Poem XVIII ("Before this loved one") takes place on mortgaged lands and is really a gesture towards an older order of things.

Rather than self-contained and argued analyses, most of the poems present incidents or situations in which behavior furnishes

---

dure. Those others, that fix themselves in the old idea, will perish with the new life strangled unborn within them."

a measurement of a class or individual's adequacy to meet the requirements of vital living. They dramatize moments of assessment, revealing encounters. When the upper class is in view, the result is an "unmasking":

> Watch any day his nonchalant pauses, see
> His dextrous handling of a wrap as he
> Steps after into cars, the beggar's envy.
>
> "There is a free one," many say, but err.
>
> (Poem IV)

Efforts to give a broader view of social conditions find in evolutionary necessity a basis for indictment. Repeatedly present is the occasion of reckoning:

> Consider this and in our time
> As the hawk sees it or the helmeted airman:
> . . . .
> The game is up for you and for the others,
> Who, thinking, pace in slippers on the lawns
> Of College Quad or Cathedral Close,
> Who are born nurses . . .
>
> (Poem XXIX)

It would be a mistake, however, to think of Auden as wholly at ease with the power of the "It" to effect a transformation. We have yet to confront the case of those hapless types whose commitment to the new life seems futile or to face the fact that even in "Paid on Both Sides," where the ideas we have been examining seem wholly in control, those of good will are defeated. "Paid on Both Sides" is a "charade," dealing with a feud between the Nower family and the Shaws, the cause of which is never revealed. It opens with news of a killing and moves on quickly to the revenge of the injured family. In an effort to end the cycle of death, John Nower proposes marriage to Anne Shaw, but the reconciliation effected is short-lived. On the eve of the wedding, Seth Shaw is taunted by his mother for failing the task of vengeance; his murder of John Nower re-opens the feud.

The influences on this play are varied—from public-school experience and the Icelandic saga, to Browning's translation of the *Agamemnon*. It has been suggested that Auden was attacking the wars of European nationalism, but this seems an interpretation too specific. For all its high jinks, the play is mainly a rendering of frustration and fatality, and the feud represents simply the harmful legacy of the past. Auden's theme is that memory—not the unconscious this time, but the ingrained influences of culture—is death, and his interest is in the necessity of breaking with forms of behavior which are self-destructive. The learned responses instilled by custom cut men off from themselves until sooner or later they realize: "these faces are not ours." It is then, in the stirrings of the unconscious, that health becomes possible:

> O watcher in the dark, you wake
> Our dream of waking, we feel
> Your finger on the flesh that has been skinned,
> By your bright day
> See clear what we were doing, that we were vile.
> Your sudden hand
> Shall humble great
> Pride, break it, wear down to stumps
> old systems which await
> The last transgression of the sea.

John Nower ponders the barren legacy of "old systems" immediately before the trial featuring the Man-Woman's accusations. When this figure appears, it is, significantly, as an imprisoned individual, "behind barbed wire." Testimony at the trial clearly points the way to release:

> In these days during the migrations, days
> Freshening with rain reported from the mountains,
> By loss of memory we are reborn,

For memory is death; by taking leave,
Parting in anger and glad to go
Where we are still unwelcome, and if we count
What dead the tides wash in, only to make
Notches for enemies. On northern ridges
Where flags fly, seen and lost, denying rumour
We baffle proof, speakers of a strange tongue.

Just as in "Since you are going to begin to-day," where it is a point of irony that those at home "call the exile fool," it is here suggested that health can be achieved only by a severance from enervating tradition—by "taking leave." And, in part at least, thinking of his own trip to Germany, Auden probably means this literally. As Spender points out, in Germany there was "youth, nakedness, lack of inhibitions, pleasure—everything which England banned."[17] We learn early that a character named Dick is leaving the country, and, later, when in fact it is already too late, John is reminded that there is still time to join him, that in no other way can one hope to overcome the heritage of the past: "We sleep in beds where men have died howling."

At the trial's end, John seems to have learned this lesson. He exits with an air of resolve, and the chorus responds with a piece, now rather ignominiously called "The Walking Tour," about abandoning the past, deliberately migrating from an unwholesome environment and, steeled against temptation and loneliness, crossing the frontier to a new land, "the old life done." There,

The future shall fulfil a surer vow
Not smiling at queen over the glass rim
Not making gunpowder in the top room,
Not swooping at the surface still like gulls
But with prolonged drowning shall develop gills.

[17] "W. H. Auden and His Poetry," *Atlantic Monthly,* CXCII (July 1953), p. 76.

The healing process envisioned is clearly immersion in the life-giving energies of the unconscious, and this poem presents Auden's most straightforward view of this solution. Remarkable in particular is the assertion that "To throw away the key and walk away . . . makes us well/ *Without confession of the ill.*" Health seems to be conceived as largely a matter of one's resolve to be well; love natural will prevail, it seems, if one can only show the necessary pluck and stamina. This assessment rings true of what we know from other sources of Auden's early attitude. He had been with Isherwood for hardly a quarter of an hour after returning from Germany before accusing him of harboring a death wish, Isherwood reports. "You've got to drop all that," Auden supposedly told him. "When people are ill, they're wicked. You must stop it. You must be pure in heart."[18] But those in "Paid on Both Sides" cannot stop: "His mother and her mother" win, and this suggests a greater recognition on Auden's part of society's persistent power than he seems to have been willing to directly express.

The attraction he felt for the sagas and for Old English poetry, however, as for the Browning version of the *Agamemnon,* argues the appeal of a life lived in obedience to deep instinctive desires. In the world of these works, men are dependent upon weather and linked to the cycle of the seasons. In Auden's "wanderer" poem, "Doom is dark and deeper than any sea-dingle" (Poem II), where the imitation of Anglo-Saxon verse is most direct, it is no accident that the call to journey is received in spring:

> . . . day-wishing flowers appearing,
> Avalanche sliding, white snow from rock-face . . .

The quest for a more vital existence is impelled by the same force melting the snow and pushing up the flowers; for individual con-

[18] *Lions and Shadows,* p. 302.

sciousness counts for little in this world: life is reduced to an elemental level and men live in the grip of processes they can neither control nor understand, but which mete out the fate they must accept. At the end of "Paid on Both Sides," the chorus exclaims that man "thinks to be called the fortunate"; but it earlier observes, "On him misfortune falls/ More than enough." It is noteworthy that to Kierkegaard "fortune/ misfortune" are categories expressing an "Aesthetic" view of existence, founded upon immediacy and thrown into confusion when frustrated from immersion in the moment.

The handling of language is another factor producing the air of human helplessness and remorseless fatality hanging over "Paid on Both Sides":

> Can speak of trouble, pressure on men
> Born all the time, brought forward into light
> For warm dark moan.
> Though heart fears all heart cries for,
>   rebuffs with mortal beat
> Skyfall, the legs sucked under, adder's bite.
> That prize held out of reach
> Guides the unwilling tread,
> The asking breath,
> Till on attended bed
> Or in untracked dishonour comes to each
> His natural death.

We may take this passage as an example of at least one of the effects Auden sought in his experiments with truncated lines and elliptical construction. The opening omission of a grammatical subject here lends credence to what the lines suggest, that man is not the controlling agent of events but the object to whom they happen; and, further, that his role of observer of events is imperfectly and almost unwillingly realized. The scanting of grammatical niceties such as the definite article and relative pronoun, with their power to precisely "place" and articulate experience, like the kennings with their insistence upon the concrete, accounts for an emphasis characteristic of early Auden, on *things,* as Jarrell notes, in their "un-get-pastable plainness"; it suggests their lack of assimilation to a purposeful mode of understanding, the experience of beings who do not yet dominate their environment to the extent of imagining themselves the point of reference for its operations. In fact, "Equipment rusting in unweeded lanes" and the like seem in Auden something removed from considerations of technology and economics, only vestiges of evolutionary error. He complains of "restlessness of intercepted growth," a phrase implying a view of life almost biological. His poems frequently take shape from processes of nature, the rhythm of the year or of daily renewal. Even personal love is represented as sharing a cyclical pattern; in Poem V ("From the very first coming down"), the "completed round" of the "year's arc" signalizes "love's worn circuit rebegun." Although the poet has been deceived in love, he must move on, "decent with the seasons."

Not history, then, but nature dominates the early work—nature not as a source of pleasure and repose or even, in the Romantic vein, as teacher of transcendent truths, but as the force behind history, as norm and natural law. Because authority is felt to lie in an appeal to the seasons, references to the time of year appear in "Paid on Both Sides" even at the cost of a violated sequence. The references occur mainly in choral pronouncements or in utterances choral in function, and they associate the ice and cold of winter with death and hostility, with the established order of things and the feud, and spring and summer with an awakening of activity auguring hope and a new life. The new life does not come in the play; the force of these images is in the juxtaposition of what men are called to do and their actual conduct:

> Often the man, alone shut, shall consider
> The killings in old winters, death of friends.
> Sitting with stranger shall expect no good.

Spring came, urging to ships, a casting off,
But one would stay, vengeance not done . . .

So the feud continues. Throughout the play and despite its confusions, the imagery works to establish a sense that when men go counter to their involvement in nature they go wrong. Bringing the thaw making migration possible, the spring opens the way to the new life. Set against the seasonal renewal of energies, human error seems discordant and misfortune ironically deserved:

The Spring unsettles sleeping partnerships,
Foundries improve their casting process, shops
Open a further wing on credit till
The winter. In summer boys grow tall
With running races on the froth-wet sand,
War is declared there, here a treaty signed;
Here a scrum breaks up like a bomb, there troops
Deploy like birds. But proudest into traps
Have fallen. These gears which ran in oil for week
By week, needing no look, now will not work;
Those manors mortgaged twice to pay for love
Go to another.

Another aspect of the appeal to nature lies in features of terrain, which typically appear in a sort of outline form, imaging almost allegorically alternatives of action or alliance. Critics have already drawn, in *The Orator's* phrase, a "map of the country" and it is only necessary to point out that the interpretative key to this lies in observable characteristics of landscape. Islands represent isolation and withdrawal because they are detached from the mainland; water conveys hope of vitality and rebirth, usually because regarded as a means of passage; mountains, because they challenge initiative and require the effort of climbing, indicate determined action or a choice in defiance of safety, and test allegiance and the ability to venture; while valleys represent the beckoning future when they are places to *be* settled—like the "happy valley" seen from the Pisgah sight of Poem XXIV ("From scars where kestrels hover"), or the entrapping past when they are sites that should properly be abandoned or *re*-settled (as in Poem XXVIII, "Under boughs between our tentative endearments," or the later "Paysage Moralisé"). Only woods stand outside this symbolic scheme, for they carry fairy-tale suggestions of dark potency and power and seem "taboo" places in the Freudian sense, which means that they elicit ambivalent feelings. Those in *The Orators* who offer a map of the country warn against a "flying trickster" in the woods and prohibit approach, but the individual who disobeys finds a vital consummation, unlike those in Poem XXV ("Who will endure") who are cowed into an acceptance of their lot by "chained-up gate" and armed gamekeeper. The ubiquitous image of the frontier brings many of these symbols together, for the frontier represents in its crossing a transition in attitudes, a shift of commitment usually from the old life to the new. Though the pattern is sometimes only suggested rather than present in full detail, there usually figures a journey across mountains from a settlement linked with the past to a new land on the other side—it is to mountains that the characters in "Paid on Both Sides" are summoned to be reborn by loss of memory. This handling of features of landscapes may be compared to the treatment of woods, mountains, etc. in the later "Bucolics." Though many of the old associations remain—mountains, for example, as the dwelling-place of types alienated from society—the play of the poet's mind with its witty analytic turns and crafty juxtapositions has become distinctive, whereas, at present, items of landscape are rarely described, only designated, as if their allegorical authority discouraged close attention. Perhaps illogically, this practice contributes in the early work to the sense of nature's dominating presence.

As in "Paid on Both Sides," however, the theme of failure plays a surprisingly large role in the poems. At times, of course, it is clearly the "enemy" under treatment, caricatured types of the sort to be observed at a sanatorium or Grand Hotel (futile refuges forming another recurrent feature of the Auden landscape) —in which case his air of clinical detachment provides an accurate gauge of attitude. This is also true when situations obviously not his own enlist his sympathies, as in "Who will endure," where a quiet irony shades into pathos. Stephen Spender has recalled how miners during the depression, for lack of anything better to do, would often pass the day sitting in bed, a practice to which the poem seems to refer as it delineates the hopelessness of a class unused to seizing initiative, who, rather than venture the necessary risk of a "Journey from one place to another," spend their time aimlessly gazing at the sea or "Leaning on chained-up gate/At edge of wood." The heritage of submission to established authority is rendered in an image of archetypal force:

> For no one goes
> Further than railhead or the end of piers,
> Will neither go nor send his son
> Further through foothills than the rotting stack
> Where gaitered gamekeeper with dog and gun
> Will shout "Turn back."

But failure is a more puzzling theme when it is the lot of less compliant types, as is often the case in poems where the element of fantasy is strong. "Control of the passes" (Poem XV), dealing with a betrayed spy, recalls the boyish imaginings described by Isherwood; and certainly it is school and O.T.C. experience, rather than the state of society at large, that is involved in Poem XII ("We made all possible preparations"), where the chief conspirators seem boys of the upper forms. Poem XXIII ("Look there! The sunk road winding") seems similarly rooted, though with a hint of more controlled meaning. As in "Paid on Both Sides," the setting is the saga world of glaciers and fortified farms; but, unlike the saga heroes, the "we's" of the poem are weak:

In legend all were simple,
And held the straitened spot;
But we in legend not,
Are not simple.

The "double beat" they will not survive to hear refers probably to the heartbeat of lovers or, more broadly, to the synchronization of individual existence with the pulsing of the life force.

There is a temptation to place these efforts most clearly deriving from schoolboy mythology beyond the bounds of solemn consideration; but to yield to this temptation would solve no problems. Social realities are so mingled with fantasy in early Auden that one cannot really discriminate two orders of experience; and even if this were possible, it would be necessary to account for the frequency with which defeat, even when more obviously located in the actual world, seems the fate of those not to be identified with the enemy. What, precisely, are we to make of the individuals in Poem XXVIII ("Under boughs between our tentative endearments") who hear the drumbeats of the future with "flushing pleasure" but still face uncertain fortunes; or of those in Poem VIII ("Again in conversations") who acknowledge the urge to a vital relationship but remain tied to an immature one? An answer is suggested, perhaps, by the fact that the problem in poems such as these is not haphazard obscurity but controlled evasiveness, a knowingness of tone implying certainty of judgment on the part of the poet, coupled with a refusal to incur outright the commitment of either sympathy or scorn. The poet opts, instead, for "clinical detachment"; but one senses in this a stratagem designed to conceal ambivalent feelings—as if, possessed by a wavering sense of identification, Auden were reluctant to choose a fate. Such ambivalence is reflected in the title from Blake later given Poem I ("Will you turn a deaf ear"), namely "The Questioner Who Sits So Sly," a title very apt, since the poem presents an unidentified voice challenging the resolve of someone, perhaps an artist, who seems to have declared an intention to remain an aloof observer of society's ills and ruses, a practitioner of exactly the sort of clinical detachment in question. The voice casts doubt on this person's ability to accept his environment without succumbing to its deceptions, insists on the difficulty of remaining uninfected in daily contact with illness, of retaining one's integrity against the urge to violence. This is aiming very high, the voice seems to suggest, asking too much of oneself, for rewards all too meagre and distant. The curious effect of the questioning is to reveal that the course indicated is a desirable one, but the questioner's position is sly indeed; for the sense of challenge, of an undertaking requiring exceptional strength and launched against odds, is not dissipated —it is as if the voice were retaining the right to reply to failure with an "I told you so."

Though to Randall Jarrell, Auden's fantasies of doom project unconscious feelings of guilt over his rebellion against authority, it would seem more accurate to recognize the thwarted rebellion and the unfree self as conscious concerns in these poems, themes deliberately if, at times, obscurely dealt with. In "Paid on Both Sides," John Nower is asked to explain what becomes of the dead —which is to say, of the past; and he replies with a catalogue of traces remaining in the present and ending: "touches of the old wound." It is precisely a "wound" that Auden's forebodings of doom seem concerned with, with the wounded state as one of undermining neurotic affliction, a remnant of "old systems" frustrating the would-be free in their effort to find the new love. A poem such as "From scars where kestrels hover" (Poem XXIV), though clearly in the class of boyish fantasy, reveals an interesting meaning if one attends to the fact that though the entire band has ventured "beyond the border" (which suggests some amount of severance from the old order), only the leader, designated "unwounded," survives this accomplishment. Presumably the others are "wounded" and perish because they are not genuinely free—like Michael Ransom in *The Ascent of F6,* whose supposedly autonomous decision to climb the mountain turns out to have been motivated by a neurotic need to supplant his brother in their mother's affections. Ransom is not the "truly strong man," nor are the "doomed companions," who are called, in fact, "Fighters for no one's sake." A fear of precisely this weakness, with regard to Auden's own companions and indeed himself, seems to underlie the poems under scrutiny: they obliquely act out unwelcome but real suspicions, voicing misgivings that "initiates" would surely have understood as anticipating the test of their own ambitions. The early poems are often fantasies conscious of their extravagance. The liberated pose and role of defiant opposition, Auden was ironically hinting, was only an indulgence of heroic longings.

The point being argued is that there are two moods in conflict during this period and that hidden dependencies, far from being unconsciously expressed, are increasingly the subject matter of this conflict. On the one hand, there is a vision of "new men making another love," an insistence upon health, an indifference to those unable to adapt and fated to die—and all this put forward with a certain bravado, with a detachment suggesting the stance of the liberated man in harmony with his instincts and indisposed to pity. On the other hand, there is an awareness that the hero's pose is a sham, that it is easier to rail against repressed desires than to seek the freedom one preaches ("the centre of anger/ Is out of danger")—that the determination to "Throw the bath-chairs right away, and learn to leave ourselves alone" represents a vain resolve. In this context, Auden's detachment operates as sour irony, as a way of conveying the bitter relish of self-mockery, as in the line, "We made *all possible* preparations." It is a way of saying: "We, too." For the point is that not only "They" but *we, too* are in bondage to old systems, are not free but wounded.

And it would be a mistake to think of Auden as coming only after a long period to this realization. The idea that salvation may be grasped simply by saying yes to Eros is not so much one the early work upholds as one it is erratically moving *away* from, one from which Auden is continually *weaning* himself as a sense of his own and his comrades' ineffectuality coheres into the recognition that they are wounded victims, unable to cast out the sins of the fathers on the strength of desire alone.

This truth is deviously confronted in *Poems,* and even in *The Orators* it is embraced almost unwillingly, but Poem XVI ("It was Easter as I walked in the public gardens") provides a rare glimpse of the underlying complexity of early attitudes, both as it is anchored in the progression of the seasons and as it comes to define the terms of the poet's relation to nature. The most explicitly personal of the early efforts, this poem is dated, it is important to note, "1929." It is a meditation upon a warped condition and a time of crisis, and it contains many of the elements we should expect. We begin with an experience of the senses in a particular locale—Germany, the public gardens; but quickly introduced is the affliction of the divided state, the burden of a reflective consciousness abstracting the individual from his surroundings. The season is spring, a time of renewal and of growing vigor, but the mood of the occasion is sustainable only so long as the poet's mind remains absorbed in his surroundings. A later passage describes the human sense of isolation as a feeling of being "Alone in flesh," facing the "otherness" of the world; even here, as an alien human presence becomes a spur to recollection, the poet's mood darkens; the scene becomes the previous winter, a time of death and failure, and his relationship with the season is dissolved. As a sudden shower falls "willing into grass," the poet is aware that he stands outside this harmonious scheme of things: human choice seems a "necessary error."

The discrepancy between tranquil nature and the individual who is at the mercy of his own development is elaborated as the human scene of "anxiety at night" is thrown into contrast with the cloud that had been moving "without anxiety" of the natural scene. Alongside the poet, for whom "living is always thinking," are the ducks, who are unself-consciously content, finding the warmth of the sun enough: "Shadow know not of homesick foreigner/ Nor restlessness of intercepted growth." We should expect from all of this an appeal to Eros and a wish for unself-conscious existence, but that is not what we get:

> Was over me in feeling without forgetting
> Those ducks' indifference, that friend's hysteria,
> Without wishing and with forgiving,
> To love my life, not as other,
> Not as bird's life, not as child's,
> "Cannot," I said, "being no child now nor a bird."

Though the decision does not come easily—is adopted indeed in a tone of manly obligation—the resolution holds, for in the third section, set in England, the "life of sheep and hay" to which the poet has temporarily returned is ruled "No longer his." He must move further from this life every hour, "As child is weaned from his mother." The point is made that, to the thwarted, love is likely to be, not the fulfillment of Eros, but its frustration:

> . . . insecure, he loves and love
> Is insecure, gives less than he expects.
> He knows not if it be seed in time to display
> Luxuriantly in a wonderful fructification
> Or whether it be but a degenerate remnant
> Of something immense in the past but now
> Surviving only as the infectiousness of disease . . .

The idea is that love cannot be free if the individual is not, that in a neurotic individual it can issue only as a form of neurosis. Auden here unequivocally places himself among the wounded. As he walks in the woods (the poem coming full circle), the thought that spring must follow the coming winter is a "forethought of death," a hope only that he will not prove "helplessly strange" to new conditions. If Love is to fulfill itself in a new order, it needs of the poet and of those like him something further than an acceptance of sex or a readiness to throw away the key and walk away:

> . . . love
> Needs more than the admiring excitement of union,
> More than the abrupt self-confident farewell,
> The heel on the finishing blade of grass,
> The self-confidence of the falling root,
> Needs death, death of the grain, our death . . .

It may seem paradoxical to assert that this notion that the old self must die is clarified in *The Orators*. This is surely the most obscure of Auden's works, one he himself described as an example of "the fair notion fatally injured." Joseph Warren Beach has suggested that "It is all written in a code, or in several codes, which one cannot hope to understand with certainty if one has not attended an English boys' school in the early thirties and acquired inside information on the 'ideology' of Auden and his intimates at this period," but even this judgment seems overly optimistic. One need only note that in a single essay Stephen Spender refers to "Marxist" elements in this work, "Fascist" elements, and, at the same time, satire on Fascism to suspect that even intimates of the period found Auden's ideology somewhat bewildering.[19] The truth is that the ambivalent feelings evident in *Poems* come to a climax in this work. The oscillation between the urge to throw off inhibitions and the unhappy awareness that inhibitions stick explodes here upon the recognition that only the healed can trust their impulses—that, as things stand, to encourage the expression of repressed desires is to encourage, not health, but a more violent form of illness. At the heart of *The Orators* is the question, "How shall the wounded be well?" and Auden's reluctant conclusion is,

[19] Spender's comments are in "The Airman, Politics, and Psychoanalysis," *The Destructive Element* (London: Jonathan Cape, 1935). Mr. Beach's remark is from *Obsessive Images* (Minneapolis: University of Minnesota Press, 1960), p. 220.

"Only by understanding their illness." It is a tantalizing and perplexing work, but with a knowledge of where Auden goes from it we can hope to realize its significance in getting him there.

It is evident from the start that the volume is written against a background of ideas essentially no different from that of *Poems*. "Address for a Prize-Day" is about "England, this country of ours where nobody is well," and the system by which the speaker diagnoses illness is Dante's, the three categories of excessive, defective, and perverted love described in the *Purgatory*. "Journal of an Airman" is also closely linked to ideas already expounded. We are told that a system organizes itself "if interaction is undisturbed," that an orderly arrangement is the "natural" result of a tension seeking to relieve itself, and that "The effect of the enemy is to introduce inert velocities into the system (called by him laws or habits) interfering with organization." The airman is a believer in the synthesis of faculties: Between center and circumference of a circle representing human personality "is awareness of interdependence." The "theories of partial priority" by which the enemy attempts to disturb this awareness are the earlier referred to "dualistic theories of a higher and lower self." Between center and center of tangential circles is "awareness of difference—love." The airman considers himself the "agent" of this awareness.

The airman is the opponent of everything in society restrictive, divisive of personality, diseased, or negative, the upholder—in intention at least—of all that is integrated and vital. He stands for "self-care," but "Self-care is not to be confused with self-regard. Self-care is care-free. Self-regard is the treating of news as a private poem." The enemy defines things by negation:

> *Unless* you do well you will *not* be loved.
> I'm *afraid* of death (instead of *I* want to live).
> Pleasure is the *decrease* of pain . . .

And the enemy fears whatever is uninhibited or suggests a confident health. "Refusal to undress in public" is an enemy trait, "don't kiss your baby on the mouth" a typical enemy prohibition. Most important, because indicating in effect the basis of the rest, is the enemy as philosopher:

> Talking of intellect-will-sensation as real and separate entities.
> The Oxford Don: "I don't feel quite happy about pleasure."

In contradistinction to the enemy idea "that man's only glory is to think," the airman's own philosophy reaffirms the concept of natural law; it is that the passions are nothing but "unreal parts" as seen by the enemy's "learned reason . . . of the unity of passion of which nothing can be said but that it is the effort of a thing to realize its own nature."

What puzzles about *The Orators* is not so much the condition of health ultimately envisioned, as the means of cure: the references to violence and to the *Fuhrer-prinzip,* the metamorphosis of the earlier conspirator figures into a fascist-type *Bund,* with an almost mystical reverence for the body and a sense of romantic male solidarity.[20] The precise significance of these elements in the prose sections entitled "Statement" and "Argument" is perhaps irrecoverable, but they reappear more manageably in the birthday ode to the son of Rex Warner, as assessment of English conditions scrutinizing the ranks of society in an effort to discover a savior for John Bull. Proletariat ("Poofs and ponces,/ All of them dunces."), upper class, youth—each is rejected until the whimsical idea occurs that the leader required is the new-born John Warner. A high-spirited account follows of his march on London, consternation among the establishment, the routing of his enemies. He will be hard on "smugging, smartness, and self-regard":

[20] I have borrowed this phrase from G. S. Fraser, who now thinks the politics of *The Orators* those of a "romantic radical of the Right," though in the 1930's he took it for granted, "as everyone did," that they were Marxist. Fraser recalls that a review in a Marxist paper denounced the ideology of *The Orators* as fascist. See "The Young Prophet," *New Statesman and Nation,* LI (Jan. 1956), p. 102, and *The Modern Writer and His World* (London: Derek Verschoyle, 1953), p. 237.

> See him take off his coat and get down with a spanner
> To each unhappy Joseph and repressed Diana,
> Say Bo to the invalids and take away their rugs . . .

And under his regime:

> The few shall be taught who want to understand,
> Most of the rest shall love upon the land;
> Living in one place with a satisfied face
> All of the women and most of the men
> Shall work with their hands and not think again.

One can say of these passages something true of many portions of *The Orators,* that though parody of a certain form or style of action is clearly present, it is so launched as to make it doubtful that the intent of this is repudiation. In "Address for a Prize-Day," the speaker is mocked as a type, but the symptoms by which he diagnoses illness are not capricious—or not, at least, to one aware that such things as a "slight proneness to influenza" or a "fear of cows" as signs of the perverted lover would not be out of place in Groddeck or that the advice to hit defective lovers in the face was pure Homer Lane. In "Journal of an Airman," seemingly inconsequential traits make up a symptomology bordering upon absurdity—but only bordering:

> Three signs of an enemy letter—underlinings—parentheses in brackets—careful obliteration of cancelled expressions.

There is evident here a shrewdness of observation that presses for acceptance; and it seems parallel that the ironic surrender to extravagance that accompanies the evocation of a *Fuhrer*-figure and informs us that we are in the presence of daydream material, fails to purge from this material the sense of a strongly felt appeal.

It is relevant to note in judging the attraction of fascist programs for Auden that by 1934 he is warning that one of the temptations for sedentary, intellectual types who stand outside the "world of action and passion with all its powers and rewards" is "to adore uncritically blood and action." Two reviews dated the same year as *The Orators* voice this appeal directly. In his "cerebral nature," man wants to "know and be gentle," Auden reminds Bertrand Russell, but in his "passionate nature man wants lordship, to live in a relation of power with others, to obey and to command, to strut and to swagger. He desires mystery and glory." And elsewhere: "Before a man wants to understand, he wants to command or obey instinctively, to live with others in a relation of power."[21] If we recognize in these Lawrentian dictums a familiar note, it is possibly because they express again the impatient yearning for an experience of vigorous life implicit in the idea of cure "without confession of the ill," the same exasperated sense of need showing through the injunction to "Drop those priggish ways for ever, stop behaving like a stone." In "Petition," Auden prays for a "change of heart" as for grace; and in *The Orators,* too, there seems present a wish for deliverance from bondage as for a transformation imposed from without.

If this suggests that *The Orators* represents a regression from attitudes expressed in the Easter-Day poem, it is true that more than anything in *Poems,* this volume reflects that "catharsis of resentment" characterizing, in Auden's view, the first achievements of young writers. But we should note that in proclaiming a man's need to command and obey instinctively before understanding, Auden implicitly recognizes that understanding is the more mature attitude. Regression though it may be, *The Orators* does effect a catharsis: Conflicting attitudes meet here in crisis, cherished impulses warring against an awareness of their immaturity; emergent maturity continuing to find in their contemplated release an appeal not easily disowned. For *The Orators* is not only *about* the death of the old self, it actually enacts this death, with

[21] See, respectively, "Lowes Dickinson," *Scrutiny,* III (Dec. 1934), p. 305; "Problems of Education," *New Statesman and Nation,* IV (Oct 1932), suppl., p. x; and "Private Pleasure," *Scrutiny,* I (Sept. 1932), p. 193.

its obscurity representing, in effect, the birth pains of the new. As before, the crux of the conflict is the "wound," the wound which justifies rebellion but incapacitates the rebel.

The wound seems to figure in isolated, unexplained statements such as "Gangrene has already set in" and in other brief references, equally obscure; but more obviously there is "Letter to a Wound," a satiric love-letter written by someone the Prize-Day orator would describe as an "excessive lover of self." If his wound is sexual in a specific sense, it is also so in the larger Freudian meaning and may be identified with any undermining attachment inhibiting mature personality growth and forcing the libido into channels of constricted development, a loss for which there are compensations. Sympathetic now to perverted elements in relationships among others, the writer has undergone the enlargement of sensibility which is one result of a frustrated libido, and for this reason and because his wound is a comfort and a protection from the challenge of self-realization, he has sentimentalized and grown to love it; the attachment will bring death, but that is more welcome than the insecurity of seeking health.

Also worth notice is the first of "Six Odes" ("Watching in three planes from a room overlooking the courtyard"), because it invokes the name of D. H. Lawrence and, like "From scars where kestrels hover," brings together mention of the wound with reference to a small group, the Auden group, and hope for a savior. The leader of that poem, in his disdain for heroism and preservation of secrecy, had shown himself the "truly strong man," one of those able to act autonomously and trust their motivations, for whom action is untainted by an insecure desire to prove themselves. Incarnations of health and invulnerable (by definition) to fears deterring the less stalwart from a realization of their deepest desires, the "truly strong" are the theoretical heroes of a philosophy of the uninhibited life; and it is likely that at some point Auden considered Lawrence for this savior's role, especially since it was a role

Lawrence often envisioned for himself. Though it is true that Lawrence was recently dead, *The Orators* repeatedly echoes him,[22] and its leader figure is also represented as having unexpectedly died. However, a somewhat different conception of the "truly strong" is important to note, one Isherwood quotes from the psychologist Bleuler: ". . . the strong individuals are those who without any fuss do their duty. These have neither the time nor the occasion to throw themselves into a pose and try to be something great."[23] Giving relevance to this observation is another Lawrence who stands behind *The Orators,* this one a hero publicly certified, but one who had renounced heroism, and who proved even more fascinating in his new role than he had previously; the new role suggested a strength in dealing with secret anxieties that called both his own former posture and that of the Nottinghamshire Lawrence into question. The conspirators, we should note, share the scholarly hobbies of Lawrence of Arabia ("Sounds of our hammers in the solemn beat of a quarry, and the packing of labelled specimens in japanned boxes"), and Auden has admitted that this Lawrence, T. E. Lawrence, was the model for "Journal of an Airman." Some verse dating from 1933 brings the two Lawrences together and suggests that at one time Auden took the idea of a leader seriously enough:

> Guilty, I look towards the Nottinghamshire mines
> Where one we quoted in the restaurants received
> His first perceptions of the human flame
> Smoky in us.

[22] The references to sun on the right and moon on the left, for example, and to belly receiving and back rejecting, derive directly from *Fantasia of the Unconscious.* Lawrence proclaims (p. 210) in this work: "The next relation has got to be a relationship of men towards men in a spirit of unfathomable trust and responsibility, service and leadership, obedience and pure authority. Men have got to choose their leaders, and obey them to the death. And it must be a system of culminating aristocracy, society tapering like a pyramid to the supreme leader."

[23] *Lions and Shadows,* p. 207.

We were to follow leaders; well we have:
The little runt with Chaplains and a stock
Or the loony airman.
We were to trust our instincts; and they come
Like corrupt clergymen filthy from their holes
Deformed and imbecile, randy to shed
Real blood at last.[24]

[24] "The Malverns," *New Oxford Outlook* (Nov. 1933), p. 148. This poem appears in *Look, Stranger!* as Poem XVII ("Here on the cropped grass"), but with this passage omitted. In light of Auden's foreword to a new edition of *The Orators* (New York: Random House, 1967; London: Faber and Faber, 1966), it can no longer be doubted that he once took the idea of following leaders seriously. Though admitting that the volume was (as I suggest) therapeutic in effect, he remarks (p. vii): "My name on the title-page seems a pseudonym for someone else, someone talented but near the border of sanity, who might well, in a year or two, become a Nazi." The foreword goes on to list some literary sources, among them Baudelaire's *Intimate Journals* and "a very dotty semi-autobiographical book by General Ludendorff, the title of which I have forgotten." Auden once made these same suggestions in a letter to me, but he there added the name of T. E. Lawrence. I don't think I have ever found the right volume by Ludendorff (until the foreword appeared, I was more than a little suspicious that Auden had been pulling my leg), though I have gleaned from the two volumes of his memoirs the observation that enemy aircraft in the First World War wrought havoc, "not so much by causing heavy casualties as by making the troops feel that they had been discovered in places which heretofore they had thought afforded safe cover"—which has a certain applicability to the activities of the airman. Baudelaire's *Journals* is a better suggestion. This work obviously served as a literary model for "Journal of an Airman," and particularly for the closing recantation. In his introduction to the Beacon Press edition (Boston, 1957), Auden suggests that the conversion recorded in "My Heart Laid Bare" involves the recognition of "the Christian concept of love as *agape,* in contrast to the Platonic concept of love as *eros":*

> He admits that to love is not to desire, however noble the object desired—even self-perfection—but to give oneself; that indeed the only way in which one can will to become oneself is by willing to give oneself in answer to the needs of one's neighbor.

Though the Christian terminology belongs to 1957, this distinction is not without relevance to the airman, who has also, in transcending "desire," attained to the service of a cause greater than himself.

T. E. Lawrence was being spoken of in the early thirties as a potential leader of Britain, and in this context he is the "loony airman" and perhaps as much as his namesake furnished material for the shadowy leader figure who appears in *The Orators*. But T. E. Lawrence's true relevance for Auden, as we shall see, lay in his retirement from public life, his repudiation of heroism; it held out a model for action distinctly at odds with the urge to follow leaders.

Certainly in its band of conspirators operating in devotion to a leader, *The Orators* is acting out the suggestion that this is a way to health, as D. H. Lawrence had proclaimed, and as was suggested too by the *Bund* movement in Germany and Gerald Heard's theory that only in the environment of communion provided by small groups (to Heard, the ideal number was twelve) could the unconscious productively blossom. In the review reminding Bertrand Russell of man's desire "to live with others in a relation of power," Auden also insists that the nation-state is "too large a unit" and explains that the attraction of communism is in its "demand for self-surrender for the isolated who feel themselves at sea." The Freudian notion that repressions are shed in a group is a complementary influence: while this *can* mean that "all the cruel, brutal and destructive instincts which lie dormant in individuals . . . are stirred up to find free gratification," Freud holds that through the domination of a leader new emotional ties may be formed and self-love given purposeful direction.[25]

Accordingly, under the guidance of the leader, the little group seems to undergo a transformation:

> Walking in the mountains we were persons unknown to our parents, awarded them little, had a word of our own for our

[25] *Group Psychology and the Analysis of the Ego*, in *Complete Psychological Works of Sigmund Freud*, ed. James Strachey (London: Hogarth Press, 1955), XVIII, p. 79. Heard's theory is set forth in *The Social Substance of Religion* (London: George Allen & Unwin, 1931).

better shadow. Crossing ourselves under the arch of a bridge we crucified fear.

Readers of *Lions and Shadows* will recognize the reference here to Auden's own group experience, the "better shadow" being undoubtedly the "Watcher in Spanish" described by Isherwood as a conscience figure. But this is no guarantee that Auden's attitude is free from irony. The prayer recited by the little group is a parody, invoking for strength, not the deity or even the life force, but detective heroes and English pubs. It reveals what it not elsewhere so certain: that Auden is indulging—and with a certain amount of ironic satisfaction and, indeed, fun—fantasies which once appealed to him and which, shared with friends, may even yet appeal, but which ultimately he cannot take seriously. In fact, though the notion of the group will continue of interest, the yearning for a healing savior is revealed to be merely another symptom of illness:

> If it were possible, yes, now certain. To meet Him alone on the narrow path, forcing a question, would show our unique knowledge. Would hide Him wounded in a cave, kneeling all night by His bed of bracken, bringing hourly an infusion of bitter herbs; wearing His cloak receive the mistaken stab, deliver His message, fall at His feet, He gripping our moribund hands, smiling.

According to Freud, the group is held together by the assurance that the leader loves all its members equally, but here the idealization of the leader is clearly neurotic; the need for his approval is so great as to be self-destructive. Like the "doomed companions," the members of the mountain band are "Fighters for no one's sake," their allegiance to a leader rooted in the condition it was meant to cure.

Only in "Journal of an Airman" is the dilemma of the wound resolved so as to render the protest against society socially effective. "Whoever possesses the instruments of knowledge, the press, the wireless, and the Ministry of Education," Auden notes at this time, "is the dictator of the country; and it becomes increasingly difficult to overthrow a bad one because imitating our voice, he makes us believe that he does not exist."[26] As one dedicated to the task of combatting dictatorship, the airman also observes that the enemy's power lies in "the people's disbelief in his existence," and his attack on two newspaper peers ("Beethameer, Beethameer, bully of Britain") is probably the most abusive piece Auden has published. The airman's enemy is disease in all its social manifestations, and his offensive is directed against those entrenched elements which, upholding the old order of things, provide the lies and diversions which blind people to their illness and prevent change. His mission to awaken the country accounts for his careful observation of the symptoms of disease and, to combat it, his three counter attacks: "ancestor worship," providing a link with the past in opposition to the established heritage to be rejected; "practical jokes," to disrupt the ingrained, conventional responses to the institutions of this heritage, breaking their hold; and "complete mastery of the air," which enables a broad, liberated view of events, counteracting enemy propaganda in the display of daring. At the same time the airman is a student of the important problem of what he calls the "real parts"—that is, the actual constituents of an integrated personality, something having little to do with the conventional enemy distinction between reason and the passions.

The airman's own release from the order of things he opposes is symbolized in his capacity *as* an airman. He is one willing to venture into new fields of experience, to "take off" from and soar above the old. It is also figured in the rejection of his paternal lineage and the selection of an uncle as his "real ancestor." This uncle died under mysterious circumstances fourteen years ago, and the airman's war against established society is in some way connected with an attempt to avenge this death. But the airman's liberation is not complete. For all his conspiratorial bravado, he

[26] Review of Dr. Maranon, *The Evolution of Sex, Criterion,* XII (Jan. 1933), p. 289.

lacks self-assurance; he is troubled by sleepless nights and a sense of isolation, and by the tormenting recurrence of a particular weakness, which some commentators have identified with homosexuality, though homosexuality, openly avowed in the second edition of *The Orators*, seems intended simply as a "given" of character of no distinctive importance. The airman's weakness, instead, is his hands, which compulsively steal. Luckily, Auden has provided a gloss on the symbolic significance of this weakness, noting in a review that the anti-social acts of criminals are a "misdirected effort to grow up" and specifically that theft is an "attempt to recover the lost or stolen treasure, love."[27] It becomes clear why the airman is "So much better when seeing E."

The airman's hands reveal, then, that he is a wounded individual and not truly free; purposeful action against the system he opposes is continually threatened by the interference of neurotic needs:

> The rose-bowl from Ardencaple still unreturned. Weak. Weak. Weak. No sooner do we succeed a little against the enemy than I let us all down, dishonour my Uncle.

All of the airman's efforts, in fact, are undermined by his hidden needs, for the lack of control over his hands only dramatizes a deeper ineffectuality. When news finally arrives that the enemy will attack, the airman finds himself incapable of deliberate action and retreats into a fantasy world of schoolboy violence:

> Banks make payment in fairy gold; girl-guides, nocturnally stimulated, mob vicars at the climax of their sermons; organists light pipes at the moment of consecration; at even-song choirs sing hymns in hesitation waltz time. Form-masters find crude graphite on their blackboards; the boys, out of control, imbibe

27 Review of Eivind Berggrav, *The Prisoner's Soul and our Own*, *Criterion*, XI (July 1932), p. 752. The second edition of *The Orators* (London: Faber and Faber, 1934) makes all pronoun references to "E" masculine, despite certain incongruities which result.

> Vimto through india-rubber tubing, openly pee into the ink-pots.

That Auden obviously delighted to write this passage need not obscure its point, which is that the neurotic individual, when he gives vent to emotion, is likely to produce only a flood of resentment, just as self-defeating as potentially destructive. Renouncing the airman's fantasies, Auden also repudiates in himself the inner impulses responsive to fascism. The danger of D. H. Lawrence, he observes a few years later, is that his advice may be read to mean simply, "Let your personal unconscious have its fling" (the insistence on "personal" is important); but, says Auden, "a piece of advice like 'Anger is just, justice is never just,' which in private life is a plea for honesty, in political life means Beat up those who don't agree with you."[28] With three days remaining till the day of attack the airman realizes that his life has been mistaken, his thoughts "suitable to a sanatorium," and that the proper course of action is revealed by the words "I have crossed it" appearing in a dream under his uncle's picture.

The reference is to the frontier, of course, to cross which is to free oneself from old encumbrances and set one's face towards the new. But a more precise meaning is disclosed by the dream, picturing E tied to a railway track on one side of a river, while the airman stands on the other, called to by spectators at a football match presumably symbolizing customary establishment values. Before events are decided, a picture of the uncle appears accompanied by his message, which in regard to himself must remain a subject for conjecture; but the words also apply to the airman's dilemma, where their meaning is clear. On the river there is a ferry boat and a ferryman whom the airman feels he has "met before, but not in real life." The river is obviously the river of death, and the uncle's message the idea once again of the Easter Day

[28] "Psychology and Art To-Day," p. 8. Actually, what Lawrence said, in his essay on Benjamin Franklin, was that *judgment* is never just.

poem that the new life requires no less than the death of the old self.

This idea the airman clarifies following his sudden illumination:

1. The power of the enemy is a function of our resistance, therefore
2. The only efficient way to destroy it—self-destruction, the sacrifice of all resistance, reducing him to the state of a man trying to walk on a frictionless surface.
3. Conquest can only proceed by absorption of, *i.e.* infection by, the conquered. The true significance of my hands. "Do not imagine that you, no more than any other conqueror, escape the mark of grossness." They stole to force a hearing.

The airman's former attitude toward his hands had been to refuse to acknowledge them part of his personality. No one was ever to know of them; by the "daily exercise of the will in trivial tasks" the affliction was to be punished out of existence. What he learns is that cure "without confession of the ill" is impossible, that he is not the "truly srong man," the "enemy" being just as much within him as without. And by this knowledge he is brought to humility ("I know that I am I . . ."); once he has accepted his hands, his plans lose their fantastic character and he is able to direct himself to immediate tasks:

> Remember to pay Bryden's bill.
> To answer C's letter.
>
> . . . .
>
> A clean shirt, collar and handker-
> chief each morning till the end.

When the day of attack finally arrives, the airman, taking off, reports that his hands are in "perfect order."

Since the airman was least effective when indulging his resentments, it is not easy to see how one destroys the enemy by ceasing to resist it. The key to this riddle is the word "absorption," understood by Auden in a specific sense and re-appearing a few years later in the dictum, "People take to violence because they haven't the strength and nerve to be absorbent." As it happens, the word is borrowed from T. E. Lawrence, about whom, in 1934, Auden wrote a brief essay, illuminating for a variety of reasons and necessary to quote at length:

> To me Lawrence's life is an allegory of the transformation of the Truly Weak Man into the Truly Strong Man, an answer to the question, "How shall the self-conscious man be saved?" and the moral seems to be this: "self-consciousness is an asset, in fact the only friend of our progress. We can't go back on it. But its demands on our little person and his appetites are so great that most of us, terrified, try to escape or make terms with it, which is fatal. As a pursuer it is deadly." Only the continuous annihilation of the self by the Identity, to use Blake's terminology, will bring to us the freedom we wish for, or in Lawrence's own phrase, "Happiness comes in absorption."
>
> But a misinterpretation of absorption is one of the great heresies of our generation. To interpret it as blind action without consideration of meaning or ends, as an escape from reason and consciousness; that is indeed to become the Truly Weak Man, to enlist in the great Fascist retreat which will land us finally in the ditch of despair, to cry like Elijah: "Lord take away my life for I am not better than my fathers."[29]

At the time this was written, Lawrence was an ordinary airman serving under a pseudonym in the Royal Air Force, and, by this transformation, at least as Auden saw it, offering the lesson that true strength lay in self-acceptance and was strength against self-deception. Clearly, "Journal of an Airman" also is an allegory of the truly weak man transformed into the truly strong, and its lesson

[29] " 'T. E. Lawrence,' " in *Then and Now* (London: Jonathan Cape, 1935), pp. 21-22; the essay is dated 1934. For the dictum on absorption, see "The Good Life," p. 39.

is the same; for as long as the airman remains unaware of the unconscious needs playing a part in his discontent, he remains driven by those needs, and his discontent must vainly spend itself. It is only when he is forced into self-knowledge, compelled to learn that his own rebellion is conditioned by the forces he is rebelling against, so that his most intense desires are untrustworthy, that he becomes a free agent. The perfect order of his hands is the symbolic indication of this transformation, but the key to the process of acceptance is understanding, that understanding betokened in the airman's new-found humility. It is only through *understanding* that illness can be absorbed, that the old self can be annihilated in the sense that its energies can be placed at the disposal of a new.

In describing self-consciousness as an asset most of us try to escape, Auden is surely criticizing attitudes of his own, and if the meaning of absorption is not clearly spelled out in *The Orators*, perhaps this is because the volume is a partial indulgence of the attitude it disowns, an expression just as much as a dramatization of the principle that those take to violence who haven't the strength to be absorbent. The new self Auden calls the Identity, a term which he promptly forsakes, but the Lawrence article leaves no doubt concerning his acceptance of the rational ego. "Action and reason are inseparable," he goes on; "it is only in action that reason can realize itself, and only through reason that action can become free." We are a long way here from the habit of mind which in Poem XIII ("What's in your mind, my dove, my coney") could refer, echoing D. H. Lawrence, to "thoughts," growing "like feathers, the dead end of life." Though Auden's fundamental tenets will prove remarkably able to assimilate the new doctrine, it signalizes a new phase in his development.

There are two epilogues to *The Orators*, though only one is actually referred to as such. Like the epilogue to *Poems*, the first is a prayer, and again, like "Petition," it is for a change of conditions that Auden hopes can be brought about without disaster by a change of heart. God is asked to "with ray disarm,/ Illumine, and not kill," and the needed change is called a necessary "defeat." The true epilogue is the ballad-like "O where are you going? said reader to rider," and since the date of its composition is unknown it may originally have been intended as a rousing appeal to throw off the old "by taking leave," except that in the place it occupies it cannot be read like that. To the first poem's assertion that we are ill and must be defeated, the second responds, "Still, we must act." The poem marks a new way of seeing things and foretells a new manner, although apparently it leaves to God the problem of evil, of defeating the will that will not understand its sickness.

CHAPTER III

Acting for Necessity

THE DANCE OF DEATH—LOOK, STRANGER!—LETTERS FROM ICELAND

Choose therefore that you may recover.
—*The Dog Beneath the Skin*

IF *The Orators* represents a catharsis and a clearing of the way for Auden, the works of the middle thirties comprise a phase of transition and re-adjustment, a seeking of more effective means to accomplish old ends, with dialectical progress towards the new values revealed by the means discovered. In Kierkegaardian terms, the transition is from "Aesthetic" values with an emphasis on powers not posited by the individual but "given" within the self and regarded as bringing into being, when fully experienced, a rich immediacy, to an "Ethical" conception of the importance of choice as a commitment of the individual to general principles. *Look, Stranger!* (1936) evidences this transition in a birthday tribute to Christopher Isherwood (Poem XXX, "August for the people") enumerating the attitudes shared by the two friends over the years. Auden recalls that when "Half-boys" their hopes were set on the "spies' career," all they observed became incorporated into an elaborate fantasy of disguises and intrigue, all their secrets were "Extraordinary and false." But five years later, they had discovered "love," that potent force which uncovers the buried self and cancels out illness:

> Surely one fearless kiss would cure
> The million fevers, a stroking brush
> The insensitive refuse from the burning core.[1]

We have noted a retreat from this conception in the early work, but by 1936 Auden is ready to write off his former hopes as irrelevant fancies. Traditional values have lost force: "Virtue" has been abandoned, "Truth dismissed without a character," "Justice" has been exiled—and what is needed now is not personal liberation but public commitment. At this time of "crisis and dismay," he asks that Isherwood's writings "Make action urgent and its nature clear."

Previous to this, the theme of disease in society had been mainly a means to impress upon the individual an awareness of his personal condition, but rejecting in *The Orators* the view that health can be grasped in defiance of upbringing and environment, Auden turns to a concern for social ills as a social problem. Though obscure private references are not entirely banished, his poetry now moves into the public world of current events. In Poem XXI ("Easily, my dear, you move"), where love is personified as a performing magician, he suggests that to ignore this world is to encourage illusion; in contrast to the old mode of fantasy, public events enter this poem with the concrete immediacy of newsreel technique:

> Ten thousand of the desperate marching by
> Five feet, six feet, seven feet high:
> Hitler and Mussolini in their wooing poses
> Churchill acknowledging the voter's greeting
> Roosevelt at the microphone, Van der Lubbe laughing . . .

The poem dismisses as a tempting conjuror's trick the suggestion

[1] Quotations in this chapter from *Look, Stranger!* are from the Faber and Faber edition (London, 1936). In the United States, this volume was published under the title *On This Island* (New York: Random House, 1937).

that personal ends may be pursued innocently or to advantage in a world no longer innocent; it enforces the awareness that anything we do involves a choice—and a choice of public significance:

> . . . love, except at our proposal,
> Will do no trick at his disposal;
> Without opinions of his own, performs
> The programme that we think of merit,
> And through our private stuff must work
> His public spirit.

It has been said that Auden now renounces Eros in favor of "selfless love," but a more accurate statement would be that *under prevailing conditions* he doubts the possibility of true self-gratification and the wisdom of seeking this end, he considers such a course likely to produce only perversions of Eros. Though the point may be theoretical, it is important to realize that love for Auden is always Eros. Even when distinguishing much later between Eros and Agape, he points out that the relationship between them is not dualistic: Agape is "Eros mutated by Grace, a conversion, not an addition, the law fulfilled, not the law destroyed." The problem is that under present conditions, and considering the force of present *conditioning*, love "cannot take that route which is straightest." He draws attention to the "large number of nervous and unhappy people who are incapable of any faithful relationship at all, in whom sensation has remained at or regressed to the infantile level as an end in itself . . . and to whom, therefore, the object is really non-existent." In such a situation, as we are reminded by a scene in *The Dog Beneath the Skin* showing the hero erotically enamored of a shopwindow dummy, love must invariably be self-regard. To say to such people that they are to trust their instincts is to learn, in words already quoted, that they are corrupt instincts and come "filthy from their holes/ Deformed and imbecile." Auden's comment on the Oxford Group Movement is to observe that tapping the "heart" can have both good and evil effects, and he has in mind the violent irrationalism of fascism. Although deeply valuing the insights of psychology, he now tends to disparage the psychologist's role. "What is the use," he asks, "of trying to remove complexes from individuals when the society into which they go demands that they should have them?" If large groups of people are incapable of meaningful personal relationships, the reason is that "Big business encourages this because human relations are bad for trade. Vitality would not keep its eye on the conveyor belt; neutors are cheaper and easier to handle."[2]

Though the admission that the instincts themselves are diseased unsettles an orientation founded upon the unconscious life force as a source of health, Auden defends his position with the distinction between the personal and the impersonal unconscious he warns against missing in the preachings of D. H. Lawrence. The corrupt instincts are those repressed by the "moralistic censor" of the conscious mind to survive in immature form in the personal unconscious ("What we call evil is something that was once good but has been outgrown"), while the aim of growth and evolution is a fulfiillment of the *im*personal unconscious.[3] His outlook re-

[2] Review of Dr. Maranon, *The Evolution of Sex, Criterion,* XII (Jan. 1933), pp. 288-89. The relationship between Eros and Agape is defined in "Eros and Agape," *Nation,* CLII (June 1941), p. 757. Auden's comments on the Group Movement appear in "The Group Movement and the Middle Classes," in *Oxford and the Groups,* ed. R. H. S. Crossman (Oxford: Basil Blackwell, 1934), p. 96. This volume of essays is particularly valuable for the light it throws on the great importance of freedom from sexual repression in the thought of Oxford students in the thirties. In an introductory essay, the Rev. G. F. Allen pictures all Oxford as suffering from shame and sexual inhibition. Supporting the program of the Group Movement, he advances the suggestion that the "forgiveness of God in Christ could work subjectively in the release of sex instincts from repression and perversion into natural health." The political view of the Movement is that the "cleansing of individual lives from acquisitiveness and fear will condition and make possible the reconstitution of the economic order."

[3] See "The Good Life," in *Christianity and the Social Revolution,* ed. John Lewis (London: Victor Gollancz, 1935), pp. 37-39, and also "Psychology and Art To-Day," in *The Arts To-Day,* ed. Geoffrey Grigson (London: John Lane, The Bodley Head, 1935), pp. 17-18.

mains centered around Eros as a life-giving force which we are obliged to satisfy; what shifts is his understanding of how this is to be done. The new insistence is upon calculated action, but it is precisely the transitional element in his thought that the goal of action is health, that his position is: "Choose therefore that you may recover." The notion that the old self must die resolves into the contention that individuals can be cured only when the form of society has been changed.

The Marxist terms accommodating this conviction are not conspicuously urged in *Look, Stranger*! The original opening of Poem XIV, "Comrades," here becomes "Brothers," and the original title, "A Communist to Others," fails to appear at all. Earlier, however, in 1933, *The Dance of Death* had appeared. It was the year of Hitler's rise to power, a time to take sides, and in the clash between Marxism and fascism the play revealed an unequivocal allegiance. Incorporated into the action is a proletarian audience issuing a call to arms blatantly unambiguous:

> One, two, three, four
> The last war was a bosses' war.
> Five, six, seven, eight
> Rise and make a workers' state.
> Nine, ten, eleven, twelve
> Seize the factories and run them yourself.[4]

Although Auden's Marxism represents a new departure and may be regarded as a turning away from personal resentments to a more objective concern with social realities, it is not as distinctive a development as it might first appear. In promising to reduce the conflict between environment and the needs of self, Marxism offers a solution to problems psychological as well as economic; it is

[4] Quotations from *The Dance of Death* are from *Poems* (New York: Random House, 1934), pp. 183-218. The original version of Poem XIV appeared in *New Country*, ed. Michael Roberts (London: Hogarth Press, 1933).

pledged, after all, to something not very different from the rule of nature, the ultimate withering away of the state. Auden's Marxism is readily assimilated into earlier views by an identification of the evolving life force with the Marxian conception of history. In his play, the dancer (who represents the death wish) is at one point a "Sun God," at whose activities the "barley and the trees grow tall," and he is described in the stage directions as both "creator and destroyer," all of which indicates that, informing the Marxist idea of "bourgeois decadence," there remains Auden's conception of the "negative inversion" of Eros, "the seed of every virtue in you, and of every deed that deserves punishment." Under other circumstances, the dancer's efforts might invite to health; it is only at present that the lure of health is deceptive:

> The young people turn to him now in their green desire
> Perhaps they imagine he'll set their hearts on fire.
> Will touch them alive as he touches the barley seed—
> Perhaps they'll find they've been very mistaken indeed.

A frankly propagandist play, *The Dance of Death* is an attack upon escapism meant to arouse enthusiasm at the inevitability of social change by revealing as futile every evasion of the responsibility to reform society. Two of these, sunbathing and summer camps, Auden regarded as diversions invented by big business as safety valves for its own protection, and, like many in the thirties,[5] he took the same view of fascist dictatorship, as suggested by the quick transition from the bathers' nudity to military uniform. Persons of influence are shown to be secretly conniving at the dancer's efforts before the play moves to modes of escape more subtly deceptive—the call to a "revolution within," suggestive of Lawrence but also allied to *Volkish* ideas in Germany, the flight of "the alone to the Alone" of religious mysticism, and, finally, dissolution, the evasive recognition that there are no evasions. The

[5] Cf. John Lehmann, *The Whispering Gallery, Autobiography I* (New York: Longmans, Green, 1955), pp. 217, 317.

time at this point is, symbolically, New Year, the place a night club named "Alma Mater," and the action a gathering of victims to celebrate their sentimental allegiance to a decadent order. But their song of celebration is, in effect, a dirge, culminating in the death of the dancer and the triumphant entry of no other than Karl Marx, who announces (to the accompaniment of Mendelssohn's "Wedding March"): "The instruments of production have been too much for him. He is liquidated."

That Marx's appearance seems more appropriate to Groucho than Karl has occasioned the suggestion that Auden did not take his Marxism too seriously, but it is easy to be too glib here; whatever the extent of his inner commitment, he was willing to publicly dramatize a message that certainly most people would have accepted at face value, and in a manner that seems extravagant only if we ignore his Brechtian views on drama. The manifesto distributed at performance[6] reads, in part, as follows:

> Drama is essentially an art of the body. The basis of acting is acrobatics, dancing, and all forms of physical skill. The music hall, the Christmas pantomime, and the country house charade are the most living drama of today.
>
> . . . .
>
> The subject of drama . . . is the commonly known, the universally familiar stories of the society or generation in which it is written. The audience, like the child listening to the fairy tale, ought to know what is going to happen next. . . . Dramatic characters are simplified, easily recognizable and over life-size.

Moreover, since drama was originally the "act of a whole community," ideally there should be no spectators: "In practise every member of the audience should feel like an understudy."

These comments suggest that Auden was writing not only for a popular audience, but for one he expected to be friendly, ready to

[6] It is given by W. A. Darlington, "A Theorist in the Theatre," *Discovery,* XVI (Dec. 1935), p. 349.

respond to his exaggerated effects and cliché-spouting characters in the spirit of partisans rallying to acknowledged truth. The scenes of audience participation obviously aim at this sort of involvement, and also accomplish some subtle effects. The presence of plural levels of dramatic illusion tends, among other things, to fix as "unreal" the dancer's activities in contrast to the "reality" of the proletarian audience. If we regard the appearance of Marx as something anticipated, the scene need not seem ludicrous, and it *is* prepared for in the sense of fulfilling a pre-determined function. As the dancer, paralyzed, dictates a will, leaving life and possessions to the working class, the chorus intersperses a resume of Western history beginning with the Greeks and Romans and working its way up through feudalism and the Reformation to the ascendancy of the bourgeoisie. These last invited the peasants into a "squalid town,"

> They put them in factories and did them down
> Then they ruined each other for they didn't know how
> They were making the conditions that are killing them now.

Marx's pronouncement that the instruments of production have been "too much" for the dancer caps this historical sequence. At the start of the play, we are invited to witness the "decline of a class" and, predictably, the arrival of Marx places this decline within his conception of the dialectic of history. Evolutionary development now appears for Auden under the guise of the class struggle.

Though *The Dance of Death* repudiates as a demogogic ruse the promise of an "English revolution suited to English conditions," Auden's fondness for his native land, like his hope that worthy elements in the English heritage will be embodied in the future, is a frequent note in the work succeeding *The Orators* and seems evidence of this volume's cathartic effect. In *The Dog Beneath the Skin*, the search for an heir happily turns up a young socialist, and in the same spirit the prologue to *Look, Stranger!* ("O love, the interest itself in thoughtless heaven") intimates that Pre-Norman tradition supports the promise of an evolving "dream," that England may yet prove an example to the continent. Auden holds out no hope, though, that transformation will be easy, for the action of the dream will not be to usher in the new life directly, but by ruthlessly excising the offenses of the old—laying on "our talk and kindness/ Its military silence, its surgeon's idea of pain." If Auden can own to a middle-class fondness for leisure and comfort, he also displays the Marxian awareness that such an attachment itself contributes to the inevitability of change:

> . . . now no path on which we move
> But shows already traces of
> Intentions not our own,
> Thoroughly able to achieve
> What our excitement could conceive,
> But our hands left alone.
> (Poem II, "Out on the lawn")

Auden's image for the waxings and wanings, more frequently, with reference to the present, for the relentless onrush of the historic process is the "flood." In *Look, Stranger!* we encounter, among other mentions, the "flood on which all move and wish to move," the "dangerous flood/ of history, that never sleeps or dies,/ And, held one moment, burns the hand," and the "crumpling flood" of social revolution which, breaking the "dykes of our content," brings death. In one of its meanings, the "disciplined love"[7] he now advocates refers to a condition of adaptability to this flood-tide of change, a willingness to forego unearned privileges and learn to live free from old dependencies. But "disciplined love" also refers to a more active commitment, to a curtailing of one's personal life and an enlightened dedication of its otherwise frustrated energies to the cause of a new order. Psychology "ignores the fact that the neurotic has a real grievance," Auden writes: instead

[7] This phrase appears in Poem XVII ("Here on the cropped grass"). I follow Mr. Beach in regarding it as a defining concept.

of attempting to adjust him to society, it should say, "Your fantasies are just, but powerless, and a distorted version of something which, if you choose to act, you can alter." In the important essay on T. E. Lawrence, he refers to the "Western-romantic conception of personal love" as a "neurotic symptom only inflaming our loneliness, a bad answer to our real wish to be united to and rooted in life":

> It is at least doubtful whether in our convalescence sexual relations can do anything but postpone our cure. It is quite possible that the way back to real intimacy is through a kind of asceticism. The self must first learn to be indifferent; as Lenin said, "to go hungry, work illegally and be anonymous."[8]

The necessity of temporary self-denial in favor of calculated action in the service of historical exigency is repeatedly urged as a solemn if, in some respects, an ironic obligation. "Our hunting fathers" (Poem III) saw in the stare of the lion the thwarted life-force ("Love") raging for the "personal glory" liberated in their own achievements, but Auden suggests that the ways of love today are not the god-like ways of liberal individualism but the "intricate ways of guilt" recommended by Lenin. Lovers today must postpone their uncertain gropings and (Poem XV, "The Chimneys are smoking") "choose the crooked" route of attacking the conditions which enslave love to uncertainty—they must serve the cause of love in concerted action. Over and over again, the poems urge the sentinel's stance and the call to duty:

> The Priory clock chimes briefly and I recollect
> I am expected to return alive
> My will effective and my nerves in order
>   To my situation.

The great enemies now are idleness, a yearning for personal glory, and—clinical detachment:

[8] "'T. E. Lawrence,'" *Then and Now* (London: Jonathan Cape, 1935), p. 22. The comment on acting against grievances is from "The Good Life," p. 47.

For men are changed by what they do;
And through loss and anger the hands of the unlucky
    Love one another.
        (Poem XVII, "Here on the cropped grass")

Paysage Moralisé" (Poem VII, "Hearing of harvests rotting in the valleys") focusses into a symbol of great and continuing importance this re-defined respect for communal effort. This sestina represents the culmination of the "map of the country" technique, playing upon familiar images of the Auden landscape. We may note as a clue to the abandonment of this technique, with its implication, however indirect, of an appeal to nature, how the images change with context to establish the "City" as the locus of human obligation and the duty to rebuild as the only means of rising above the blight identified in stanza one as the "sorrow." In this stanza, starving cities are the image of this sorrow, mountains are barren, grain rots in valleys, water and islands suggest only shipwreck. A clue to this bleak state of affairs is furnished by the second stanza. Unlike those made helpless by misfortune, the original founders took action against their sorrow, crossing mountains, seeing in valleys the promise of learned cities; now, in connection with the founders' purposefulness, all key words have positive value—water is something craved for and found, islands introduce the notion of rescue.

Stanza three, establishing a symbolic tension between cities and islands, provides the crux of the poem's meaning. Cities have failed to satisfy the longings of the inhabitants, whose sorrow is assuaged only by dreams of departing for islands where mountains and valleys promise utopian contentment; and cities and islands now vie with each other as the proper site of human endeavor. In the following stanzas, islands win out,[9] but the poem operates by set-

[9] The confusing misprint "their sorrow" in stanza five is corrected to "your sorrow" in *Collected Poetry*. The image of the visiting sea god is another recurrent in Auden, expressing right through *The Age of Anxiety* the vain hope for a golden age or happy isle. But the *New Country* version of "The Chimneys are smoking" seems to intend this association

ting up a symbolic opposition whose values are the reverse of those held by the characters within the poem: Cities are symbolic of man's practical efforts at fulfilling his aspirations, while islands are fantasy settings dreamt of at night. It is the escapist surrender to an illusory goal, which, rather than the "learned cities" of stanza two, has produced the "starving cities" of stanza one and transformed the metaphysical sorrow of stanza three into actual loss:

> So many, doubtful, perished in the mountains
> Climbing up crags to get a view of islands;
> So many, fearful, took with them their sorrow
> Which stayed them when they reached unhappy cities;
> So many, careless, dived and drowned in water;
> So many, wretched, would not leave their valleys.

The longing for Eden is all the more deeply our "sorrow" because those who succumb to the dream do not believe in it. The conclusion places the poem's two major symbols into proper relationship. The release of sorrow would be fertilizing: we would "rebuild our cities, not dream of islands." In light of the resemblance between the sorrow and the "wound," one could not ask for a more explicit reversal of the early hope that health might be achieved by taking leave.

Though readers of the thirties would have seen in Auden's reiterated appeals for disciplined effort the Marxist reference they were intended to, this new emphasis on constructive action, by virtue of the importance it accords to the privilege of choice, evidences an outlook in the making as much at odds with the Marxist conception of history as with early prescriptions for health. The lovers of Poem XVI ("May with its light behaving") reject the consolations of personal love because they have moved from the "vague woods" into the "real world" of injustice and death. They stand "with shaded eye,/ The dangerous apple taken," and for

---

without irony; the line "like a sea god the political orator lands at the pier" here reads "communist" in place of "political."

this reason purposeful action lies open to them. That such action depends on the power of self-consciousness Auden admits in the article on T. E. Lawrence. The significance of the admission is to open the question of the free human will. Does the life force stipulate the form of its own fulfillment or is this, by virtue of the "dangerous apple," the prerogative of human decision? Is there only history-nature or is man a creature of nature with a power of his own to create history? Although Auden is not yet ready to face these questions definitively, we have noted the assertion that "love, except at our proposal,/ Will do no trick at his disposal." If this is so, the value which he must place on the role of the self-understanding ego becomes critical indeed. "Psychology is fundamentally a rationalist movement," he writes:

> It does not say, as some, like D. H. Lawrence, have been inclined to say, "Trust your instincts blindly." Just because it believes that the exercise of the reason is the only way through, its first task is to show how little the reason is able to effect directly. Nor does it deny the possibility of free will, except in a sense which is also true of Christian theology. Just as the theologian says that every man is fallen and in bondage to Satan, so the psychologist says that everyone is neurotic, at the mercy therefore of his repressed impulses, and unable to escape from his image. At the same time his aim is to release his patient through increased self-knowledge, so that he may really exercise his reason and make a genuine choice.

He ascribes to art and psychology the same function—"not to tell people how to behave, but by drawing their attention to what the impersonal unconscious is trying to tell them, and by increasing their knowledge of good and evil, to render them better able to choose, to become increasingly morally responsible for their destiny."[10]

Not surprisingly, he now refines his strictures on the type of

[10] "Psychology and Art To-Day," p. 18. The long passage preceding is from "The Good Life," pp. 39-40.

mentality the airman had formerly attacked in such gibes as that "to think" was the enemy's idea of man's only glory. This mentality implies a doctrine of dualism, "of the higher and lower self," he re-asserts; but he now sees that it rests upon a belief in "character," which "presupposes a belief in the superiority of the will over all other mental faculties." This is the "conscious will, the will of the ego," but his criticism is directed not at the will's dependence upon thought but at the *disinclination* to think, at the "policy of actively resisting evil without too much thinking, for thinking by threatening the initial premises may bring the whole structure down in ruins."[11] A table that he draws to illustrate the features of three periods of history identifies as the twentieth century's "Worst Sinner" the "deliberate irrationalist," and as the best means of realizing the good life on earth, "Self-understanding." Bringing to an interest in fairy tales his remarkable talent for finding parables in the familiar, he suggests that the youngest son of the tale succeeds partly out of "good nature" and partly because he deals with problems "by understanding rather than with force" (later he will change his mind about this). The table entry that perhaps sums things up, under the heading "Personal Driving Forces," reads "The unconscious *directed by reason*."[12] Although he will accept and begin to exploit fully this new recognition only after a time, it is clear that "disciplined love" refers to Love Rational, and that the "self-forgetfulness" he continues to preach now means the capacity to free the self from hidden compulsions by the exercise of this power. Disciplined love, self-forgetfulness, freedom

[11] "The Group Movement and the Middle Classes," p. 91.

[12] The table may be found on pp. 14-15 of "Psychology and Art To-Day," the comment on the fairy tale in the footnote on p. 6. In Auden's later view, the fairy tale hero succeeds because of freely-given Grace, a conception which, curiously, seems more applicable than that quoted to the hero of Poem XI ("Just as his dream foretold"), who finds aid thrust upon him. "Which was in need of help? Were they or he/ The physician, bridegroom and incendiary?" the poem asks. The occupations reflect the fact that heroes are supposed to restore health, purge corruption, and marry princesses.

—they all rest, in Engels' words, on the "consciousness of necessity."

It is as a consciousness of necessity also that "nature" still remains an illuminating conception. In evolutionary terms, Auden was attempting in *Poems* to see as the "hawk" sees or as the "helmeted airman." But the main effect was a sense not so much of distance as of immense pressures and impending turmoil, for in technique as well as outlook, and despite the pretense of clinical detachment, the early work tends to depreciate the ego's perspective as it stands apart ordering its observations. Delmore Schwartz has remarked that the imagery of islands, mountains, etc. seems to conceal "a residue of undigested meaning": nature dominates not only because man is contained *in* nature but because its dark processes resist his comprehension. In the present period, this is no longer so: individuals and their problems appear as social phenomena to be analyzed in historical terms; things are now "reduced to nature" in the special sense of being understood and assigned their place in an intelligible progression.[13] The analysis of social ills as a consequence of industrialism in "Here on the cropped grass" is an example of this. More developed is the survey of history in *The Dance of Death*, with its emphasis on the economic factors causing the rise and fall of civilizations. Poem XXVII ("Fish in the unruffled lakes") exploits the contrast between animal innocence and human guilt, anticipating Auden's fully developed handling of what is essentially the old "Chain of Being" idea. The survey of history may be regarded as a horizontal counterpart to this, a "Chain of Becoming" in effect, enforcing the consciousness of necessity by placing the present in relation to the shaping processes of the past.

The extended vistas common to many poems also serve to dis-

[13] Auden has said that, from "10,000 feet, the earth appears to the human eye as it appears to the eye of the camera; that is to say, all history is reduced to nature." See "Hic et Ille," *Encounter*, VI (April 1956), p. 36. Delmore Schwartz's comment appears in "The Two Audens," *Kenyon Review*, I (Winter 1939), p. 38.

tance and lend perspective to the confusions of the present. It is to express an outlook that Auden writes from the "cropped grass of the narrow ridge," "England below," or from the "narrow window of my fourth floor room," or notes that the "Great Bear/ Hangs as a portent over Helensburgh." References on the geological or cosmic scale, to England as "perched on the edge of the Atlantic scarp," to the planets as they "rush towards Lyra," serve the same purpose.

Language in the early work had been terse, highly dependent upon ellipsis and a wrenched syntax, and the poetry had been largely the result of these effects; but in the present period, where that foremost example of the ego's organizational talents, the City, first appears as a symbol,[14] language too more and more comes under intellectual control. We may note developing the Audenesque style characterizing many of his most anthologized pieces, one based upon long, heavily clausal sentences, syntactically complex but conspicuously grammatical, with their full complement of compound verbs and objects. A new technique of imagery indicates an attempt to find a means of objectifying abstract notions. In its simple form, the technique may be noted in the capitalized personifications of "August for the people," but it is present also in similes of a surrealistic quality such as

> . . . for the long lost good,
> Desire like a police-dog is unfastened;

and it may be extended in detail:

[14] I follow Joseph P. Clancy—"Auden Waiting for his City," *Christian Scholar,* XLII (Sept. 1959), p. 187—in citing "Paysage Moralisé" as Auden's first full use of the City as symbol. Actually, the passage in *The Dance of Death* beginning "We shall build to-morrow/ A new clean town" reveals the same conception, and the use may even go back to "Paid on Both Sides," to the passage "There is the city,/ Lighted and clean once . . ." I have never been sure whether the reference of this image was external or internal, but the passage in either case seems to be a first, Auden's first use of what Spears calls "psychic geography" if not of the city as symbol.

> The presses of idleness issued more despair
> And it was honoured,
> Gross Hunger took on more hands every month,
> Erecting here and everywhere his vast
> Unnecessary workshops . . .

Although not sensuous, these figures can be visualized, and often not until then are they fully grasped; based upon purely conceptual resemblances, they have the diagrammatic quality of the editorial cartoon.

It is important to realize that though Auden's new outlook demolishes the old, it continues to build upon the same foundations. Not only does he retain respect for Homer Lane and his teachings (some of the most forthright expressions of the view of illness as purposive and as a perversion of the basic energy of love appear in the choruses of *The Dog Beneath the Skin*), he continues to hold what he identifies as the common view of Marxism and psychology that "thought and knowledge" are not something "spontaneous and self-sufficient, but . . . purposive [like illness, though more effectively] and determined by the conflict between instinctive needs and a limited environment." Although he insists that psychology does not reject "self-consciousness and reason," that both psychology and Marxism believe "attempts to put the clock back, either in economic or psychical life, are reactionary and dangerous," and that psychologists will be needed after society has been changed (indeed, that is *when* they will be needed), self-consciousness and reason seem important at present mainly because "everyone is neurotic, at the mercy therefore of his repressed impulses" or, alternatively, of the hidden motivations of class interest. It is noteworthy in this connection that there is a distinct difference between what he recommends to his own contemporaries and what he hopes for future generations. This point is best exemplified by Poem X ("Now from my window-sill I watch the night"), where he imagines himself under the scrutiny of a strange pair referred to as "Lords of limit," who, "setting a tabu 'twixt left and right," are preservers of order and punish its violation. These figures have been recognized as of Apocalyptic origin, but it has not been noted that the relevant *Apocalypse* is D. H. Lawrence's, where they are described as "gods of limit, each forever jealous of the other, keeping the other in bounds," and identified as "the two alternate forms of elemental consciousness, our day-consciousness and our night-consciousness."[15] Following a hint of Lawrence's, Auden invokes the two as guardians against Saturnalian excess, the excess of fascist irrationalism, and represents his own generation as needing their discipline, able to pass muster only by deliberate effort and disguise. For his pupils, however, he envisions a more vital integration, in terms recalling his definition of the ideally "cured" individual as "one in whom the unconscious and the conscious were at one, and who would obey his impulses":[16]

> Give them spontaneous skill at holding rein,
> At twisting dial, or at making fun,
> That these may never need our craft,
> Who, awkward, pasty, feeling the draught,
> Have health and skill and beauty on the brain.

Discipline is the means by which one chooses to recover, but its function is to prepare for a time when it will no longer be needed.

That discipline is necessary at present, however, acts to restrain Auden's hopes. It is significant in this respect that impersonal denunciations of the doomed are no longer so scathing as they once were, in fact are no longer impersonal. Poem XII ("As it is, plenty") satirizes the successful individual determined to overlook his surrender to the system and the betrayal of his own ideals, but not without a sense of pathos, if not futility. Another castigation of self-interest (Poem XVIII, "The sun shines down on the ships at

[15] *Apocalypse* (New York: Viking Press, 1966), pp. 129-30.

[16] Auden's views as quoted in this paragraph are from "The Good Life," pp. 39-40, 46, and from "Psychology and Art To-Day," p. 19.

sea") evidences a resigned irony supporting the suggestion that this sin is universal. In general, that split in the treatment of illness or inadequacy between *their* "self-regard" and *our* "wound," between the doomed and the saved, obscurely enforced in the early work, is hardly apparent. "Out on the lawn" explicitly acknowledges Auden's own inability to rise clear of his class.

Doubt and an uneasy conscience provide a quiet counter-statement to the insistence upon determined action which is the dominant note in *Look, Stranger*!—and they betoken an assessment not long quiescent. The epilogue re-invokes the old We-They dichotomy, but in contrast to those such as Lenin, Freud, and Groddeck,

> Who pursued understanding with patience like a sex,
>   had unlearnt
>   Our hatred, and towards the really better
>   World had turned their face,

Auden groups himself with "Us," and this seems more than a rhetorical concession. "Can/ Hate so securely bind?" the poem asks; "Are they dead here?" and it answers: "Yes," for Auden confronts here the unlikelihood that men can act in defiance of their wounds so as to transcend the old pressures towards malice and illness. To accept Love Rational is to accept a principle defined by its capacity for error, and Auden's rejection of his early reliance on a spontaneous blossoming of Eros carries so far that he envisions a contending principle and adopts temporarily the Freudian conception of the death wish and the corollary that hate is real. The human problem is to make constructive use of hate, and he admits that for the masses as a whole he knows of no method other than war by which this may be accomplished.[17] In Michael Ran-

[17] "The Group Movement and the Middle Classes," p. 100. Despite his lack of enthusiasm for the movement itself, Auden (p. 98) is in accord with the importance it places on small groups: "Only in a group of very moderate size, probably not larger than twelve, is it possible for the individual under normal circumstances to lose himself, for his death instincts to be neutralized in the same way as those of the separate cells

som's cry in *The Ascent of F6*—"Save us, save us from the destructive element of our will, for all we do is evil"—this pessimism reaches its extreme. Ransom's agreement to climb F6 is delivered as an indication of the autonomy of his will operating independent of his disdain for his brother, but he soon finds himself tempted in his exploit by pity for the sufferings of the ordinary. Like the renowned figure of Poem XIII ("A shilling life will give you all the facts"), he is not the "truly strong man": what presents itself as a desire to "save" these people really manifests a need for adulation, the same need to outdo his brother in their mother's eyes prompting the original decision. At the end, the "Demon" that corrupts the will is revealed to be Mrs. Ransom, and the Abbott tells us, "If there were no Demon there would be no temptation." In the play's view, the will is evil because people are neurotic; but this is a diagnosis, not a solution.

Letters from Iceland (1937), a travel book in prose and verse written with Louis MacNeice, though it provides further evidence of dejection and doubt, also reveals the role of these factors in shaping new and more resilient values. "Journey to Iceland" describes the futility of hoping to find relief on this island from the cares of Europe: the "fabulous Country" is "impartially far," for here too the blood moves by "crooked and furtive inches" and justice is lacking. But the volume contains also the witty and thoroughly enjoyable "Letter to Lord Byron," a poem in five parts best described as a response to the question, "Who am I?"[18] and pursuing an answer by means of a survey of the time in diverse

---

of the metazoa neutralize each other in the body." This idea is explored in *The Orators*. The mention of the cells alludes to a passage in Freud's *Beyond the Pleasure Principle,* as does a similar passage in "Here on the cropped grass"; see *Complete Psychological Works of Sigmund Freud,* ed. James Strachey (London: Hogarth Press, 1955), XVIII, p. 50.

[18] I am indebted for this suggestion to Professor William Cadbury. All quotations from *Letters from Iceland* (London: Faber and Faber, 1937; New York: Random House, 1937) are from the British edition.

areas of experience, as well as in the autobiographical effort to portray "An intellectual of the middle classes" in Part IV. Among other things in this deliberately rambling poem is a characterization in fairy tale imagery of the hero who has replaced the old swaggering John Bull as the figure of English man. To see him, says Auden, "Turn to the works of Disney or of Struba" (in "New Year Letter" it will be Thurber):

> There stands our hero in his threadbare seams;
> The bowler hat who straphangs in the tube,
> And kicks the tyrant only in his dreams,
> Trading on pathos, dreading all extremes;
> The little Mickey with the hidden grudge . . .

"Heroes are sent by ogres to the grave," the little man tells himself: "I may not be courageous, but I save"; but Auden refuses to accept this platitude. The little man dreams of one day slaying the ogre, but if he were no longer oppressed he would be deprived of his dream: "He dreads the ogre, but he dreads yet more/ Those who conceivably might set him free." Auden displays little hope here in a social revolution accomplished by the masses.

Yet his tone is not desperate but sure and rather tranquil, and the poem suggests a modification of expectations accompanied by a certain shifting of sights. He identifies himself (or, at least, tells us that his friends identify him) not as a Marxist, but as a "selfish pink old Liberal," and a great deal of his fire is directed at the tyranny of officialism and efficiency, a theme developed in the forties and later dominant. The age is "highly educated," he informs Byron—"There is no lie our children cannot read"; and he exclaims against that "Goddess of bossy underlings, Normality!" At the end of the poem, although he reiterates his belief that thought is the product only of a "complex" or of a lack of material satisfaction, he seems resigned to the divided condition. Blake's fine idea of a marriage between Heaven and Hell "won't take place":

The Great Utopia, free of all complexes,
The Withered State is, at the moment, such
A dream as that of being both the sexes.

But the thought is consolatory that the highest human achievements originate in repression, and he is now capable of adopting as a slogan: "Let each child have that's in our care/ As much neurosis as the child can bear." It has been said that *Letters from Iceland* expresses Auden at his most despondent, but such a judgment overlooks the paradox that despondency was generating a kind of strength, that once again the problem of evil—of the fallen will, enslaved to neurosis, to concealed self-interests, to habit, but enslaved only because possessing the power to be free—was forcing a more complex and rich evaluation of the human condition.

This situation is best revealed in the "Letter to R.H.S. Crossman," for this poem of self-criticism presents him deliberately seeking for something positive to lighten the burden of guilt and disillusion causing him to see in a glacial flood the image of "history, hostile, Time the destroyer" and to think truly human only the "anarchist's loony refusing cry" that no choices are good. Auden confronts here "the hands, the feet, the faces," acknowledging his desire to see "the growth, the wonder" rather than "symbols of an end . . . Of a tradition sick at heart." The poem treats of the necessity for a renewal of vision, an appreciation of the uniqueness of individuals and events as justification for faith in humanity. It is our "vulgar error" to remember only the "formal interdiction from the garden," the loss of unself-conscious innocence occasioning our struggle for law and order, and to forget the "rusting apple core we're clutching still," attesting to choice and our potential for goodness. Auden and MacNeice close their "Last Will and Testament" with a prayer that the "good" who have been tempted to withdraw may be granted power to assume the "guilt" of action and the insight to acknowledge that they must labor for a goal, the City, destined to imperfection; but neither concession undermines the faith in human resources they announce as a credo:

> Believing man responsible for what he does,
> Sole author of his terror and his content.
>
> The duty his to learn, to make his choice;
> On each the guilt of failure, and in each the power
> To shape, create and move, love and rejoice.

If the outlook displayed in this passage is substantially that of *Journey to a War* and later works, we may take this to indicate the transitional nature of this period, which effects a change in values not so much by altering programs and principles, as by modifying the expectations on which they bear. For a portion of the time certainly, evolutionary forces shaping history more or less according to the pattern envisioned by Marx constitute for Auden the "unconditional" which we are obliged to heed. Since it is not clear, though, that the pattern is strictly pre-determined, implementation requiring human decision and action, and raising the question of the freedom of the will, he is forced to make do in the last analysis with the more ambiguous conception that our duty to Eros lies in choosing to bring into existence a more satisfying form of society. The fact is that his position is peculiarly *ad hoc*. The proper means of human development he may describe as "The unconscious directed by reason," but his thinking is not yet fully alive to the implications of choice, because he tends to regard his own generation as unique and abnormal. Even *Letters from Iceland*, suggesting that the good cannot act without guilt, conveys the attitude that this is particularly a phenomenon of the thirties. The greater his pessimism, however, the more complex his sense of human possibility, for the effect of this mood is to make innocence appear irrecoverable and imperfection an inescapable and distinctively human attribute. There is during this time an attachment to the hope that *after* reason has established the just society, man may regain obedience to the law of his own nature and recover something not remote from "The unself-consciousness/ That children share with animals" ("Letter to Lord Byron"), but as this hope recedes, it becomes possible for Auden to recognize in his respect for the human power to reason and choose a suggestion of richer values, and the foundations of something more than an interim philosophy. The recognition is hastened, if not actually caused, by his growing awareness of the true menace represented by fascism. Because the recognition arises from an acceptance of the divided condition, it enables a full appreciation of the human freedom deriving from this condition. Although the concept of health continues to dominate Auden's thinking in the mid-thirties, it yields after that to the concept of freedom.

CHAPTER IV

The Questing Ego

IN TIME OF WAR—ANOTHER TIME—NEW YEAR LETTER

> . . . the daemonic powers are helpless
> by themselves, since it is the day life
> that must not only find the means to the
> ends they desire, but even discover the
> ends themselves. For the Unconscious is
> blind; it knows it wants something but
> cannot tell what it is until the right
> something is put into its hands.
> —"Jacob and the Angel"

IN the mid-thirties, fascism appears in Auden as a phenomenon of mainly psychological interest, a symptom of illness, and, like all such symptoms, an attempt to effect a cure, by bringing to the surface desires long repressed by society. Like the airman's fantasies, it does not actually accomplish cure, for its irrational release of energies leaves untouched the real source of illness, which is capitalist society itself, with its foundation in production for the sake of the few, its class-conscious morality and suppression of real spontaneity, its need for servile workers to man the machines. By allowing pent-up resentments noisy but ineffectual expression, fascism relieves some of the stress of illness, but it also acts for the status quo; its net effect is to strengthen capitalism. This view is expressed not only in *The Dance of Death* but as late as 1938—in a third theatrical collaboration with Isherwood, *On the Frontier*. Depicting a war between Ostnia, which resembles England, and fascist Westland, the play sides with those enlightened enough to recognize the real source of their grievances, the workers in both countries who refuse to fight and, in fact, rise against their governments. Between Ostnia and Westland there is little to choose. Fascist dictatorship is portrayed as a capitalist ruse for keeping the people in check by the device of a "national martyr."

Putting aside the anachronism of *On the Frontier,* this assessment of fascism is not the one we now encounter. Whatever its psychological significance, by 1937, with civil war raging in Spain and Japanese armies advancing into China, with Germany thriving on a program of militancy, fascism stood revealed not as an evasion to be rejected but as an international threat, a political force with a philosophy of its own, to be opposed in the cause of freedom. Psychological understanding remains, of course, valid, and Auden continues in the role of diagnostician. Poem VIII from *Another Time* ("It's farewell to the drawing-room's civilized cry") has been found perplexing because, though satirizing dictatorship, it attributes to the devil the disorderly forces occasioning the dictator's dementia; the point is that as repressed desires seeking release these must be acknowledged dangerous; in Poem XXIV ("Where do they come from"), they are the "Terrible Presences" expressing "our need for forgiveness" in the form of armies massing for war, just as in "Spain 1937" invading battalions are "fever's menacing shapes." But psychological analysis has little bearing on the political issues at stake as illness reaches its crisis. Totalitarianism battens on the frustrated urge to health and, offering the many a release from decision and personal restraint, a mindless health, at the expense of freedom, its effect is to force a choice of values. Auden decides that freedom is a more precious possession than health, that it is a privilege actually rooted in the nature of our humanity. Fascism must be opposed so that we may choose, not to recover, but to evolve.

The emphasis in "Spain 1937" on the struggle, the moment of decision on which the future rests, is relevant in this connection. The poem has been called Auden's last effort to make a Marxist of himself—a description more accurately accorded to *On the Frontier*—but Marxists were disturbed by its reference to "the flat ephemeral pamphlet and the boring meeting," and there is more in the poem than politics warrants. We would like to turn to Eros as to a *deus ex machina,* Auden observes, to have it resolve our problems as it arranges the lives of the creatures. But he suggests that to the human species Eros functions only as an accomplice:

"O no, I am not the Mover,
Not today, not to you. To you I'm the

"Yes-man, the bar-companion, the easily-duped:
I am whatever you do . . ." [1]

The point here is not only that crisis has been reached but that the unconscious is blind, that our capacity for choice, far from being a useful ally in a time temporarily out of joint, is the indispensable means by which Eros seeks to know its goals. Vindicating the ego's susceptibility to error, a consequence of freedom, this view gives meaning to the divided condition from which freedom arises. Contemplating this condition, Auden is now willing to suggest that conflict within the self is perhaps a law of our being: "Heaven and Hell. Reason and Instinct. Conscious Mind and Unconscious," he writes, and then asks whether the antagonism of these factors "constitutes a temporary and curable neurosis, due to our particular pattern of culture," his early view, or whether, in fact, it is "intrinsic to the nature of these faculties?" He speculates that the Socialist State will "marry" the opponents but quickly adds: ". . . perhaps it won't . . . Perhaps the only thing which can bring them

[1] Unless otherwise mentioned, quotations from Auden's poetry in this chapter are from the American edition of *The Collected Poetry of W. H. Auden* (New York: Random House, 1945) rather than the British edition (London: Faber and Faber, 1948). "Spain 1937" was first published independently (London: Faber and Faber, 1937) and then reprinted in *Another Time* (London: Faber and Faber, 1940; New York: Random House, 1940).

together is the exercise of what Christians call Charity."[2] As hinted here, Auden's "liberal" or "humanist" convictions, though they will survive the change, are no less transitional than his Marxism had been. The antagonism between ego and self is ultimately a wrestling bout enacted within the individual, and, having defined the terms of human development, he will be forced to confront its personal implications. But this is to look ahead too quickly. At the time that concerns us, his preoccupations were public in nature, and a reasoned conception of human development was highly relevant.

This conception appears in *Journey to a War* (1939), a collaboration with Isherwood treating their experiences in China, and particularly in "In Time of War," a sonnet sequence with a verse commentary which identifies the true peril of fascism as its threat to freedom and to the humane values made meaningful by freedom. The sequence expresses the view that freedom is man's right and obligation because, as a creature whose evolution is incomplete, he must "find" his nature. This is the point of the survey of evolutionary and historical progress found in the "Commentary." References to man's upright posture and his civilizing efforts, to his emergence from holes in "the warm sunshine of the Laufen Ice Retreat," the rather grand acknowledgment that "the growth of the fore-brain has been a success"—all of these place in the perspective of a continuous struggle to develop our goal of "*Jen,* the Truly Human." Seen in relation to a process stretching back into unrecorded time, the issues at stake in China reveal their enormous importance: For "the creature who creates, communicates, and chooses,/ The only animal aware of lack of finish," the defence of freedom is a struggle to maintain the foundations of human identity.

Analyzing our present condition by putting it into relation with prior determinants, Auden suggests that the seeds of fascism

[2] "Jehovah Housman and Satan Housman," *New Verse* (Jan. 1938), p. 16.

were sown with the Renaissance, which, preparing for the subjugation of the instincts imposed by industrialism, saw self become a private world, divorced from the one exposed by reason in which the body performed its mechanical tasks. In an important essay called "Jacob and the Angel,"[3] he explains that we are now witnessing the end of the Protestant era, "during which the day life and the night life were segregated from each other. On one side was the humanist tradition of the Renaissance, expecting a millennium for the practical and social man through the exclusive use of the individual reason; on the other was the Calvinist tradition of the Reformation making the contemplative man, whether as artist or as religious, the passive instrument of daemonic powers." In Romantic political theory, the doctrine of Grace, as the theory of the General Will, became a social principle, but it was not until after the first World War that political Romanticism emerged as a force to be reckoned with:

> Romanticism grew with Industrialism: for that very day of work and money which is essentially the domain of conscious and willed acts, has, with the growth of centralization, specialization, and mechanization, taken on more and more, for the vast majority, the arbitrary determined aspect of the night and the dream, and not a pleasant dream either. For how many millions is their free individual life now thrown back into a Personal Unconscious . . .?

The hypnotic tones of fascism, which people hear as the call of "Instinct," represent, he explains, really a cry of frustration, the "wailing of an egotistical 'Reason' crippled by inaction." And to surrender the day life to this cry is only to further betray our humanity. In the Commentary, he pleads that the heart be made again *"awkward and alive,"* but he expressly denies that men can regain the primal condition. To the fascist cry that *"Man can have Unity if Man will give up Freedom,"* he rejoins, *"Men are not in-*

[3] "Jacob and the Angel," *New Republic,* CI (Dec. 1939), pp. 292-93.

nocent as beasts and never can be";[4] the ideal to which he summons allegiance is a "human justice."

If the sonnets uphold this ideal in terms often journalistic, their directness of manner can be attributed to a background of war threatening an end to human advance. At the same time, they stress a hopeful point, the doctrine of "Hongkong," that "For what we are, we have ourselves to blame." Auden indicates the widespread area of guilt—the lack of justice which is general, the aloof unconcern of the democratic powers; but a tempering influence is the realization that the opportunity for error is essential to the truly human, that if man has failed to achieve the Just City, his capacity to seek out the good and shape his destiny at least makes the City an intelligible goal. The order of the twenty-seven sonnets is perhaps not immediately apparent; they divide into four groups, each with an aim of its own despite a general forward movement. Beginning with Creation and the Garden, Sonnets I-III have the function of defining man's nature, and their point is that, by virtue of his freedom, it is something he must define himself; the next group (Sonnets IV-VIII) take up his effort to do so, examining his principal occupations, while Sonnets IX-XII are transitional, treating historical developments parallel in importance to the war in China dealt with by the remaining poems.

Establishing a "he" able to change shape in time and then tracing the process of metamorphosis, the sonnets give the history not of men, but of *Man,* the species, the shifting pronoun reference signifying the truth implied by his evolution through the ages: "Nothing is given: we must find our law." The Chain of Being technique in Sonnet I discloses this uniquely human obligation by the process of distinguishing the fixed capacities of other species: Bee, fish, and peach all "knew their station and were good for ever"; only man is "continually mistaken," although by his capacity for error, since it enables a quest for truth, he is set above the

[4] Quotations from *Journey to a War* (New York: Random House, 1939; London: Faber and Faber, 1939) are from the American edition.

other creatures. The price he pays for the power to choose is (Sonnet II) expulsion from the garden, the fall into self-consciousness creating his sense of sin, but also enabling the freedom which he finds "wild," because self-consciousness, disrupting instinctive responses, cancels the primal oneness of unself-conscious life. By the process which placed him "outside of" nature, man became in effect the creator of his world. With the development of language (Sonnet III), he became a bestower of values able to differentiate his experiences and choose among them; as a result, no longer the slave of Love Natural, he was subject to his own conventions: He "shook with hate for things he'd never seen,/ And knew of love without love's proper object."

The skills and resources developed by man are the subject of Sonnets IV-VIII, which treat him as, respectively, farmer, soldier-knight, philosopher-scientist, poet, and merchant. Though a strict progression between these roles is not intended, history is provocatively incorporated *within* the poems by an effect of anachronism casually produced by the introduction of contemporary terms of reference. The result is that the first tiller of soil (Sonnet IV) is transformed into a bovine type appealing to oppressors, and the adventurous medieval knight (Sonnet V) into a Miniver Cheevy who rankles in offices. Resources invaluable in one age but inconsequent to the needs of another act out their shift in value: contemporary affairs are placed in the perspective of a historical development which they also comment upon.

Sonnet IX, which might be called "Ancestors," suggests that we in the present betray "the kingly and the saintly" of the past by refusing to give life to the heritage passed on to us. It asserts our dereliction of the "Truly Human" and opens the next group treating the three "Great Disappointments" that have occurred in the quest for human unity—the failure of institutionalized Christianity (Sonnet X), that of the Roman Empire (Sonnet XI), and finally (Sonnet XII) that of "Empiric Economic Man," as he is called in "New Year Letter." His failure, our own, is exemplified most notably by the war, comprising the subject of the next fifteen poems.

Here the struggle to make man man is localized; and by bypassing on the whole the conflict of nationalities and reducing the struggle to the naked opposition of elementary values, Auden asserts that since the fault lies with man, so it lies with each of us. Evil, Justice, Truth, Wrong, Freedom—these "ethical" concerns are the issues and the adversaries, and if they bring to mind the fulsome speeches heard by Lieutenant Frederic Henry in *A Farewell to Arms,* Auden's point, really, is that we are now paying for the disillusionment of the twenties; our failure is the irony of supposing these things fictions. Irony as a rule inheres in the disparity between the actual and a sense of fitness which the actual violates; it reflects our trust in a moral universe. But here Auden reverses the process; the war reveals that the universe *is* moral, that responsibility for our actions means we get what we deserve:

> Yes, we are going to suffer, now; the sky
> Throbs like a feverish forehead; pain is real;
> The groping searchlights suddenly reveal
> The little natures that will make us cry,
>
> Who never quite believed they could exist,
> Not where we were.
>
> (Sonnet XIV)

The effects wrought by war are unambiguous: the terror of the victimized, the homelessness of refugees, the anguish of the injured. The response the sonnets require of us is equally so. Auden is alive to the ironies of war's normal operation, the soldier "Abandoned by his general and his lice," the serenity of embassies where lives hang upon a slip in phrasing; but unremittingly these ironies are made to dramatize the pressing reality of the issues the war represents. Maps upon the office wall in the perfectly symmetrical structure of Sonnet XVI represent only the "idea" of war, whereas the *reality* on battlefields is different: men "thirst at nine who were to thirst at noon,/ And can be lost and are, and miss their wives." But Auden insists that "ideas can be true although men die":

> And maps can really point to places
> Where life is evil now:
> Nanking; Dachau.

Returning to the contrast between primal innocence, the "warm nude ages of instinctive poise," and our own lives, the concluding sonnet asserts that "We live in freedom by necessity"; we are apprentices, "articled to error."

Auden is not always forthright, however, in espousing the values of liberal democracy. Seeking a sense of the unconditional, he is reluctant at times to make too great a claim for values many might argue to be arbitrary or relative. The principle of "health," of instinctive needs of the human organism unconditional in the sense of "given," had been founded upon the authority of "nature." A noteworthy element in his effort to place "freedom" on an equally authoritative basis (by showing that human nature is defined in our choices) is the implication frequently present that freedom is a principle as unambiguous, theoretically, as health—the marked reluctance to assert that the good life also requires allegiance to values according to which freedom is exercised. Thus, an essay published in 1938 and reprinted the following year in *I Believe,*[5] a volume collecting the personal credos of prominent men, argues the conception that the moral exercise of freedom consists chiefly in enlarging the area over which freedom is enjoyed.

The essay distinguishes between good and evil as "natural" and as "moral" qualities, a distinction employing the antithesis between necessity and freedom later more elaborately surveyed un-

[5] *I Believe,* ed. Clifton Fadiman (New York: Simon & Schuster, 1939); originally, this essay was "Morality in an Age of Change," number VII of the "Living Philosophies" series, *Nation,* CXLVII (Dec. 1938), pp. 688-91.

der the categories Nature and History.[6] A thing or creature is good, Auden begins, "which is discharging its proper function, using its powers to the fullest extent permitted by its environment and its own nature":

> . . . an organism is *naturally* good when it has reached a state of equilibrium with its environment. All healthy animals and plants are naturally good in this sense. But any change toward a greater freedom of action is a *morally* good change.

It is possible to speak of a favorable mutation as a morally good change, but it is one spontaneously achieved; for creatures below man the only good possible is again natural good. But man differs from the animals in that changes in his nature are not dependent upon genetic mutation: "an animal which has reached maturity does not continue to evolve, but a man does"; and, in man, "the evolution can be continued, each stage of moral freedom being superseded by a new one." Although moral goodness will pass into natural goodness with each advance (the life of the peasant once represented the "highest use of the powers of man," but "People committing acts in obedience to law or habit are not being moral."), and although each advance will increase the opportunity for moral evil as well as for good,[7] "moral progress" is possible. It

[6] Auden first uses these terms in opposition in "The Poet of the Encirclement," *New Republic,* CIX (Oct. 1943), pp. 579-81. They denote a distinction essentially between necessity and freedom and have many precursors: after the distinction between "natural" and "moral" qualities in *I Believe,* the opposition appears (in the notes to "New Year Letter") as that between "Causal necessity (Fortune)" and "Logical necessity (Virtue)," in the distinction between "tribulations" and "temptations" attributed to Kierkegaard (see note 17), and in the difference drawn now from Henry Adams, though not employed much until later, between the world of the "Dynamo" and that of the "Virgin." Since the distinction is fundamentally a projection into the objective world of the subjective separation between ego and self, it parallels that between body and mind, Sancho Panza and Don Quixote, Caliban and Ariel, etc.

[7] Natural evil consists in "Determined and unavoidable limits to freedom of choice and action, such as the necessity for destroying life in

consists in the increasing expansion of man's freedom, a process accomplished by the exercise of knowledge: "By studying the laws of physical nature he has gained a large measure of control over them and insofar as he is able to understand the laws of his own nature and of the societies in which he lives, he approaches that state where what he wills may be done."

The remainder of the essay attempts to give these thoughts practical application. Democratizing Plato, Auden decides that a society is good when it allows "the widest possible range of choices to its members to follow those vocations to which they are suited" and when it is "constantly developing, and providing new vocations which make a fuller demand upon their increasing powers." Our politics will depend upon the extent to which we think badness in society preventable. If we are "fairly optimistic, believing that bad environment can be changed, we shall tend toward a belief in some sort of democracy."

Auden declares that he himself is fairly optimistic, but it is noteworthy that badness as he conceives it here is ultimately equivalent to lack of knowledge, a deficient "consciousness of necessity" preventing us from extending our freedom so as to establish equilibrium with our environment, and that underlying this position is the "Ethical" view—and, as Kierkegaard describes it, the "Ethical" error—that to know the good is to will it.[8] This view is predicated on an assumption of the ego's autonomy, at least potentially; if in the chain of being man is, as "New Year Letter" has it, "Half angel and half *petite bête,*" it assumes that the will can provide for his creatureliness as pure understanding directs. To be sure, Auden

---

order to eat and live, climate, accidents"; but "Just as moral good tends to pass into natural good, so, conversely, what was natural evil tends, with every advance in knowledge, to become moral evil." (*I Believe,* p. 4) The italics in the passage set off in the text are mine.

[8] See in particular "The Socratic Definition of Sin," in *The Sickness Unto Death.* Unlike Auden who prefers to schematize and sharply divides Religion from Ethics, Kierkegaard points out that this is the view of *pagan* Ethics.

is not always philosophical upon this point—one of the notes to "New Year Letter" reads: "To know the Good, you say, is to will it?/ But with some the immediate reaction is: Kill it." But this poem continues to associate evil with lack of knowledge, and this notion Auden will not fully relinquish until he experiences the force of Reinhold Niebuhr's demonstration that man's greatest temptation to sin inheres precisely in his paradoxical situation as a being half in and half out of nature.

Both *Another Time* (1940) and *New Year Letter* (1941) reveal a significant shifting of interests—a lessening of concern with Eros as an abstract force and greater respect for the individual relationship with Eros which each ego must experience in relating to a particular self. The poetry of the early years had been, though not personal in character, highly private, almost to the point of being exclusionary, and throughout the thirties, in repudiation of this, the swing is towards an utterance more and more public, both in manner and viewpoint. Now, in viewpoint, the pendulum begins to reverse. Five days after the invasion of Poland, Auden in a review of Rilke is at pains to defend that writer's withdrawal from the passions of the First World War:

> This tendency is not to be dismissed with the cheery cry "defeatism." It involves not a denial of the importance of political action, but rather the realization that if the writer is not to harm others and himself, he must consider, and very much more humbly and patiently than he has been doing, what kind of person he is, and what may be his real function. When the ship catches fire, it seems only natural to rush importantly to the pumps, but perhaps one is only adding to the general confusion and panic: to sit still and pray seems selfish and unheroic, but it may be the wisest and most helpful course.[9]

Although *Another Time* furnishes little evidence, in any intimate sense, of the kind of person Auden is, it is the first of his volumes

[9] "Rilke in English," *New Republic,* C (Sept. 1939), p. 135.

to contain in any quantity poems not in direct response to contemporary social conditions and, also, occasional verse, putting "conditions" into the background to reflect intellectually upon particular events. We can see in this migration from warnings, prophecy, and appeals, all rendered useless by the arrival of war, not only a broadening of horizons and a freeing of intellect to range afield, but the opening of an inquiry into the individual and his search for meaning. The volume shows a far greater range in both subject and tone than any previous. One section is given over to "Lighter Poems," among them "Refugee Blues" and "The Unknown Citizen," somber enough thematically; also here are the exuberant, if insufficiently funny, "Three Ballads": Illustrating the theories of Homer Lane, repressed "Victor" becomes homicidal, his heartless father succumbs to heart disease, the priggish "Miss Gee" develops cancer.

Another Time contains, too, many of Auden's most interesting and celebrated efforts: "Musée des Beaux Arts," "September 1, 1939," "In Memory of W. B. Yeats." In addition is a whole group of poems treating the lives of famous writers and thinkers, mainly from the past, many of whom Auden would be pleased to regard as "ancestors" within the humanistic tradition. They are those such as Voltaire, Melville, and Freud who have helped us to evolve or, in more common terms, who have civilized us. If on the whole these poems offer little that is new on the problem of divided consciousness, like "New Year Letter" they indicate the breadth of interest appropriate to a concern with the truly human and the expanding role of intellect in examining this conception, aided by insights from the social sciences and other disciplines. We have grown used in academic criticism to judging poems by evocativeness of imagery and language—poetry's capacity to express the conflicting strains of a rich response to reality as unified experience. Most of these poems, however, succeed in a way we are less adept at handling—by bringing diverse particulars under the hold, not of an experience which the reader is made to share, but of an intellectual relationship that he must consider and assess. They require of the critic an appreciation of the process by which things are named so as to be given a role in a conceptual order based upon judgment and understanding, of poetry's power to interpret and clarify experience so as to make it a vivid intellectual possession. "Musée des Beaux Arts" strikes the imagination because it discovers in Brueghel's painting the force of an idea, just as, in the Freud poem, richness of observation derives from the power of understanding to seize from complicated matters an essential simplicity. In the following passage, poetic appeal lies not in what imagery, by stimulating association, draws *into* the poem, but in analogy's power to formulate *out,* out from the intangible, a precise conception:

> He wasn't clever at all: he merely told
> The unhappy Present to recite the Past
> Like a poetry lesson till sooner
> Or later it faltered at the line where
> Long ago the accusations had begun . . .

As with that of the Yeats elegy, this poem's ability to organize our feelings springs from the judiciousness it manifests in articulating and assessing our public debt, from the authority established by intellectual cogency. Important here is not what the poem *is,* but what it *does.* What "September 1, 1939" *does* is to formulate the claims of conscience for a dazed generation, putting this generation (and the imaginatively sympathetic reader) into possession of its experience by an act of understanding. John Blair is right to characterize Auden as "anti-Romantic" and to note his affinities with eighteenth-century poetry;[10] as he indicates, Auden needs a

[10] This position is expounded in *The Poetic Art of W. H. Auden* (Princeton: Princeton University Press, 1965). For an excellent analysis of "In Memory of W. B. Yeats," see Robert Roth, "The Sophistication of W. H. Auden: A Sketch in Longinian Method," *Modern Philology,* XLVIII (Feb. 1951), pp. 193-204.

criticism less concerned with surface texture than with the larger patterns of wit, judgment, and conceptual understanding.

Another feature linking Auden to the eighteenth-century is the Chain of Being technique, present all through this volume and probably, from this point on, the conceptual construct most frequent in the poems as they examine nature so as to define the human situation and explore the human awareness of time and the freedom to choose creating history. The hourglass may whisper to the lion's paw (Poem XV), may even blunt it, as Shakespeare's nineteenth sonnet suggests, but the lion and the rose "Care only for success" and always achieve it. Nature, being nature, cannot err; only self-conscious man has difficulty being himself, prefers "some going round/ To going straight to where we are," and experiences the complications of living in time. Auden acknowledges this with a bemused satisfaction, for the unself-consciousness of animals is an ideal now only by way of analogy. If the poem called "The Creatures" accepts these beings as "our past and our future," it insists that we may "more generously recover" the pride of their ways by the exercise of "Charity."

If we recall the remark that "what Christians call Charity" might unite the divided self as the socialist state could not, it will not seem surprising that Auden now finds in the creatures a clue not to the nature of love, but to that of evil, which he will soon unequivocally define as arising from self-love. In a sense, of course, this is not a new equation: the neurotic "self regard" hindering an understanding of true motives and needs (like the material self-interests which rally unobserved to the threat of change) express a destructive self-love. But now vaguely, and later conclusively, the reference is to something inherent, a corruption of will, originating not in illness or fear, but in nature. "Nature/ Can only love herself," we are told in "Oxford"; the difference is that in a self-conscious being self-love is no longer, as with the creatures, innocent; it is what Christians call Pride. Considering our failure to prevent the war, Auden reflects that what Nijinsky wrote about Diaghilev is true of the *normal* heart:

> For the error bred in the bone
> Of each woman and each man
> Craves what it cannot have,
> Not universal love
> But to be loved alone.
> ("September 1, 1939")

There is, of course, an inconsistency here with the more optimistic notion that evil is the result of faulty knowledge. Faulty knowledge, Auden will come to hold, is itself often the result of a blinding and innate self-love. Meanwhile, it is noteworthy that his oscillation between the two conceptions mirrors that other wavering we have observed between allegiance to the broad ideal of freedom and specific commitment to values made meaningful by freedom, such as justice and charity. The issue at stake in both cases is the fallen will, and for Auden it will be resolved by the revealed truths of Christianity, Protestant Christianity, with its insistence on the depravity of man's nature and the need for Grace. Interestingly, he tells us that his conversion was prompted by a vivid dramatization of the will's inability to subdue a raging self: "I was forced to know in person what it is like to feel oneself the prey of demonic powers, in both the Greek and Christian sense, stripped of self-control and self-respect, behaving like a ham actor in a Strindberg play." In the later "Canzone," these words are partially echoed:

> In my own person I am forced to know
> How much must be forgotten out of love,
> How much must be forgiven, even love.

If our love, too, is tainted, then the pursuit of more and more freedom, far from being an unconditional, really constitutes a license to evil, a denial of unconditionals. Widespread before the war, this denial, Auden will decide, was also its cause: "... man cannot live without a sense of the Unconditional: if he does not consciously walk in fear of the Lord, then his unconscious sees to it that he has something else, airplanes or secret police, to walk in fear of."[11]

An extended analysis of the modern situation in relation to the war, "New Year Letter" is not nearly so blunt. It represents a last attempt to do without belief in God, to continue to find sufficient cause for awe and obligation in Eros; and in some respects it shows the strain of this effort. In the United States, the poem appeared in a volume called *The Double Man,* and since the point of this study is that, in a sense, the double man is the theme of *all* Auden's work, Richard Hoggart's suggestion that this is the more suitable title[12] is difficult to resist. The poem decides that unified being may be experienced only momentarily, that human existence is a continual "becoming," and that by a "double focus" of faith and doubt the ego in each of us must pursue a solitary quest for self-fulfillment as governed by natural law. But these things will be clear if we take the poem on its own terms, and towards this end, and towards an understanding of poetic method, its actual title is indispensable. "Letter," suggesting an unceremonious meditation, prepares us for the air of "reverent frivolity" encountered, the freedom of reference and allusion, and the discursive bent, as "Letter to Lord Byron" had acknowledged, common to letters: "I want a form that's large enough to swim in,/ And talk on any subject that I choose." "New Year," on the other hand, reveals the orientation organizing Auden's material. Instancing our customary celebration of the New Year, Kenneth Burke has said that "the human

[11] "Tract for the Times," *Nation,* CLII (Jan. 1941), p. 25. For Auden on his conversion, see his contribution to *Modern Canterbury Pilgrims,* ed. James A. Pike (New York: Morehouse-Gorham, 1956), p. 41.

[12] *Auden: An Introductory Essay* (London: Chatto & Windus, 1951), p. 160. Like the London edition of *New Year Letter* (Faber and Faber, 1941), *The Double Man* (New York: Random House, 1941) gives notes to the poem not reprinted in *Collected Poetry.*

mind is prone to feel beginnings and endings *as such*."[13] The poem testifies to this, arguing that "the machine has now destroyed/ The local customs we enjoyed," that with the war a "whole system . . . Shudders her future into stone," that Marx is now "one with those/ Who brought an epoch to a close." It asserts of those fighting in Europe:

> . . . each one knows
> A day is drawing to a close.
> . . . .
> That all the special tasks begun
> By the Renaissance have been done.

We live, Auden believes, at the end of the Protestant era or, as he has it here, the Renaissance, and the poem is his analysis of the factors bringing this era to disaster and of the situation we confront in readying ourselves to set out anew.

The poem, in other words, is about death and the necessity for rebirth, the rebirth, in "Epithalamion's" words, "Asked of old humanity," and this theme is reflected in diction and imagery when it observes that art is not "A midwife to society," or when it pictures the devil as a celebrant of the womb, or explains that some dreamed the Russian revolution had realized "potential Man,/ A higher species brought to birth/ Upon a sixth part of the earth," but that, though the "rays of Logos" take effect, "dwarf mutations are thrown out/ From Eros' weaving centrosome." Bringing an epoch to a violent close, the war is the death incurred for having failed our task; it is a parody birth issuing, like Miss Gee's cancer, to protest a reality frustrated. Europe lay trembling in apprehension, "As on the verge of happening/ There crouched the presence of The Thing":

> All formulas were tried to still
> The scratching on the window-sill,

[13] *Counter-Statement* (Chicago: University of Chicago Press, 1957), p. 139.

All bolts of custom made secure
Against the pressure on the door,
But up the staircase of events
Carrying his special instruments,
To every bedside all the same
The dreadful figure swiftly came.

The pressure so steadfastly resisted by formulas and the tightened bolts of social rigidity is actually projected, of course, by a stifled unconscious, and it is to superintend the release of this force that the surgeon figure, Time, arrives. "We would rather be ruined than changed," thinks Malin in *The Age of Anxiety.* It is a consistent point with Auden. If we cling to the past and refuse to change, with the coming of time the unconscious makes our changes for us.

Though the direction of the poem is towards a fresh beginning, a new Re-naissance, no such rebirth actually occurs:

Our news is seldom good: the heart,
As ZOLA said, must always start
The day by swallowing its toad
Of failure and disgust.

Despite this repellent inversion of the birth image, the poem concludes with a prayer, a request for guidance. As has been said in parallel circumstances of *The Waste Land,* it moves toward a point outside itself, this being Auden's decisive acceptance of Christianity. In shaping this end, the poem does contemplate rebirth as an experience of regenerative contact with the unconscious; in religious terms again reminiscent of Eliot, it affirms the possibility of a moment out of time when we touch upon eternity, "Unconscious of Becoming," and from which we depart "Obedient, reborn, re-aware." The obligation to transform our lives is reenforced, though we still face the problem of how to do so.

As a means to organizing analysis, the poem's three sections each concentrate on a period of time reaching its close at the New

Year; the first part focusses on the climate and aftermath of the war year, 1939, the second ("Tonight a scrambling decade ends") upon issues raised by the thirties, the third on broad developments since the start of the Renaissance. In addition, each of the sections is unified by what Kenneth Burke would call a "representative anecdote," a projection of man in a particular stance revealing the section's chief preoccupation. Though brought to the surface by imagery, these imaginative constructs are not really sources of organization, evoking a symbolic response, but emblems of an organizing view in force independently and active throughout. Like the imagery of birth objectifying the thematic implications of New Year, their function is mainly to bring to the attention an intellectual orientation and make possible the play of wit as inquiry proceeds. Part I, then, may be entitled "Man Under Judgment," Part II "Man and his Devil," Part III "Man as Seeker of the Way."

The first section measures the disorder of contemporary circumstances—hatreds crystallized into "visible hostilities"—against the ideal order possible in art and reaches the conclusion that we stand indicted and have much to atone for. It is not that art can teach us to be good, for "Art in intention is mimesis/ But, realised, the resemblance ceases"—art presents "Already lived experience" and shapes its materials into an order of its own, different from "Life-order," which is the task of living men. But the order of art still constitutes a judgment upon us, as a paradigm of the possible. As poet, Auden admits that he has sinned against his craft. And evoking the theme of man under judgment, he imagines himself tried for his misdeeds by a "summary tribunal" of dead masters, the presiding judge, it is interesting to note, being Dante and an associate magistrate, Blake. As "ancestors," these represent a poetic conscience, and Auden confesses that he has been careless and hasty in his work, he has adopted the "preacher's loose immodest tone." But a greater offence is murder, that of a civilization plunged into the havoc of war. Here judgment requires some detective work:

The situation of our time
Surrounds us like a baffling crime.
There lies the body half-undressed,
We all had reason to detest,
And all are suspects and involved
Until the mystery is solved
And under lock and key the cause
That makes a nonsense of our laws.

The "Whodunit" analogy is cleverly elaborated, and the conclusion is that "guilt is everywhere."

"Man at the Crossroads" might be a subordinate title for Part II, which formulates his role as "Seeker of the Way" with an image of an indecipherable signpost on a barren heath, roads branching ahead in all directions and the ruins of the old order behind. But since Auden's chief interest is in the errors bringing us to an impasse, tendencies of mind, this section belongs to the devil, the tempter who split man's consciousness and encourages error. More than a lively personification, the devil is Auden's means of portraying the results of the Fall. This section is really an analysis of the privileges and perils of self-consciousness, and a last effort to account for evil as a deficiency of knowledge. It concedes that our knowledge must always be defective and perhaps in this takes an important step towards the Christian view that evil is inherent in man, but it also offers the hopeful observation that the devil's true function is to "Point us the way to find truth out," that in his flashy legerdemain lies the gift of "double focus." As we should expect, Auden starts from the premise that love is the animating force of the universe. If this is true, then "Evil is not an existence but a state of disharmony between existences"—there really is no devil:

. . . for all your fond insistence,
You have no positive existence,
Are only a recurrent state
Of fear and faithlessness and hate,

That takes on from becoming me
A legal personality . . .

Indicative of the direction in which Auden is moving, the key word here is "faithlessness"; the devil represents mainly doubt, though not of the kind confronting the limitations of human knowledge with a healthy skepticism and, indeed, frustrating the devil; doubt, rather, is here a want of faith in ultimate order, an anxious response to the estrangement from order caused by the Fall, taking the form of an impatient reaching for absolutes. We are told in the notes that the devil's philosophy in all its varieties begins in dualism. Since evil is disharmony, it is any philosophy of one-sidedness that fractures the whole so as to exalt the part, and its manifestations are distortion, oversimplification, inflexibility—all those practices representing flight from the insecurities of existence by a resort to the false certainty of extremes.

Directed since the Fall towards the goal of "Rule-by-sin," the devil's temptations indicate the solemn result of self-consciousness: our ability to do evil consciously. In the poem's words, to sin is to be aware of violating harmony, "to act consciously/ Against what seems necessity." And since all creatures are parts of the whole, sin, like evil, entails acting "contrary to self-interest":

> It is possible for all living creatures to do this because their knowledge of their self-interest is false or inadequate. . . the animals whose evolution is complete, whose knowledge of their relations to the rest of creation is fixed, can do evil, but they cannot sin.
>
> But we, being divided, remembering, evolving beings composed of a number of "selves" each with its false conception of its self-interest, sin in most that we do . . .[14]

But if self-consciousness makes sin possible, it also makes possible efforts to lessen disharmony and the goal of "Diversity in unity." It

[14] Prose quotations pertaining to the devil are from the "Notes" section, *New Year Letter.*

is the devil's dilemma that, though sin requires an awareness of our interests, this awareness also works against sin; and the result is that, "torn between conflicting needs,/ He's doomed to fail if he succeeds." In championing a particular bias, the devil is undermined by the capacity of a self-understanding being to know his values relative:

> . . . If there
> Are any cultures anywhere
> With other values than his own,
> How can it possibly be shown
> That his are not subjective . . .

While if he plays the god and establishes an absolute, eliminating the awareness of alternatives, he destroys the foundations of his own existence, reducing us to the status of animals, capable of evil but not of sin, "A possibility cut out/ In any world that excludes doubt." The devil's only recourse is to try the impossible, "To be both god and dualist," and this means that, while continually active, he must resist pushing his efforts to a self-defeating conclusion and, thus, must run the risk of educating his victims.

All this is a flat summary, with the aid of the notes, of what is briskly and wittily dramatized in the poem. On the level of particulars, the devil's stratagems are varied and shrewd; he is the partisan not only of all extremes but of the full about-face, as in the case of Wordsworth, whose conservatism was the result of failing to find in the French Revolution the "Parousia of liberty." Observe to the devil that the categories of intellect are barren abstractions, "that we,/ In fact, live in eternity," and he will shift from the opposing position with unctuous grace:

> . . . when with overemphasis
> We contradict a lie of his,
> The great Denier won't deny
> But purrs: "You're cleverer than I;
> Of course you're absolutely right,

I never saw it in that light,
I see it now . . ."[15]

The danger of the devil is that he will encourage our individual tendencies to one-sidedness and then convert the correction of disillusionment into the reaction of despair, but our protection lies in the paradox of his position: anchored in our own nature, "he may never tell us lies,/ Just half-truths we can synthesize."

Summarizing the implications of this view, Part III marshalls resources for a confrontation with the future. It is the longest and most historically encompassing of the three sections—but not so long as to prevent a clear expression of most of what it has to say in images of landscape and, in particular, in the image of man in endless forms seeking his temporal Way along the slopes of Purgatory. The Renaissance conqueror of nature, "Empiric Economic Man," could "drive himself about creation/ In the closed cab of Occupation," but the corresponding images of today show Kafkas of the laboratory puzzling over "the odd behaviour of the law," "The path that twists away from the/ Near-distant CASTLE they can see," and the *Völkerwanderungen* by which Americans explore that freedom to change their fate won by bringing to a conclusion the work of the Renaissance. Today, the search for a Way is an obligatory venture over open ground, an individual Quest:

Each salesman now is the polite
Adventurer, the landless knight
GAWAINE-QUIXOTE, and his goal
The *Frauendienst* of his weak soul . . .

[15] The Faber and Faber text of "New Year Letter" gives an erroneous end-quote after the phrase "clever than I." This probably accounts for Francis Scarfe's mis-attribution of the devil's speech to the poet himself, and his consequent misreading (*W. H. Auden,* Monaco: Lyrebird Press, 1949, pp. 43-44). Curiously enough, Richard Hoggart (*Auden,* pp. 163-64) makes the same error and ascribes to Auden a disposition in favor of heart over intellect inconsistent with the poem's principle of "symmetry."

Landscape in this section, in addition to furnishing symbolic settings (and allegorizing Auden's opinions as shaped by youthful experience) defines the relationship between the individual and society: "Maps and languages and names/ Have meaning and their proper claims," Auden asserts. He argues that there are "two atlases," one identifying the inner world of self, "the place/ That each of us is forced to own," the other the world of public affairs in which we work and act: "Where each one has the right to choose/ His trade, his corner and his way."

The New Year actually arrives in this section, accompanied by the reflection that this "*Annus* is not *mirabilis*": "Our road/ Gets worse and we seem altogether/ Lost." It had been implied, earlier, by the indecipherable signpost. But if the goal of the Quest is not in sight—the Just City for society, for the individual his fulfillment therein—the section does acknowledge that rebirth of purpose which comes from an experience of union with unconscious life-sources nourishing all our strivings:

> . . . it happens every day
> To someone. Suddenly the way
> Leads straight into their native lands,
> The *temenos'* small wicket stands
> Wide open, shining at the centre
> The well of life, and they may enter.

During such moments, the split in consciousness is healed: immersed in "free rejoicing energy," we have regained the garden where freedom and law are one. Our problem is that we cannot live there: ". . . perfect Being has ordained/ It must be lost to be regained." A refusal to be subject to time and continual Becoming brings a drastic change of landscape: "The sky grows crimson with a curse,/ The flowers change colour for the worse," the wicket padlocks itself. And Heaven becomes Hell, the state of suffering of all who refuse to accept suffering as a necessity and consequence of living. Mountains in early Auden had been barriers to cross on the way to a life of aesthetic immediacy; but he now contends that we are a mountain people, that we live on Purgatory, where we must suffer and will our salvation, "Consenting parties to our lives."

It is still with a reliance on natural law, however, that he considers our terrain negotiable, for the notes tell us that there is a "Natural Way" and that the attitude of the seeker must be one of faith and doubt: "Faith that Natural Law exists and that we can have knowledge of it; Doubt that our knowledge can ever be perfect or unmixed with error." This long-standing faith in natural law Auden will soon surrender, deciding that "If the commands of God were laws *of* men, then disobedience would be impossible"; they are instead the "call of duty, 'Choose to do what at this moment in this context I am telling you to do.' "[16] At present, however, his category of inquiry is still the evolutionary one of "Man in Society," and "New Year Letter" retains a secular hope in the Just City as a state of equilibrium, continually enlarging, with environment, considering the individual's existential quest mainly in terms of an abstract freedom won by society from nature.

In an article,[17] Auden points out that on the tribal level, where the pressures of nature are intense, freedom means little more than "the privilege to be alive," that it is only when control over natural

[16] *The Living Thoughts of Kierkegaard,* ed. W. H. Auden (New York: David McKay, 1952), intro., p. 16. For Auden's first statement on the untenability of a theory of natural law, see "The Means of Grace," *New Republic,* CIV (June 1941), p. 766.

[17] "The Means of Grace." The distinction referred to in this paragraph between temptations and tribulations is given in *New Year Letter* ("Notes," p. 132) as follows: "As far as I know, Kierkegaard was the first to distinguish accurately between *tribulations,* all the troubles that come upon us from without and can't be disposed of by acts of will but can only be endured, that is, treated aesthetically; and *temptations,* all the internal conflicts that must not be endured but solved in action by the will, that is, treated ethically. Further he was the first to include among tribulations, not only physical disasters like flood, fire, and famine, but also all images, impulses, feelings of guilt that rise from the subconscious."

forces improves, lifting the power of external necessity, that it becomes clear that "the life of the individual and the life of his community are not identical and that freedom is not only the freedom to live, but the freedom to live one of several possible lives." This development may be attributed to "Empiric Economic Man," who in his subjugation of nature brought under the control of moral will what were before events only to be endured as "tribulations":

> . . . he broke
> The silly and unnatural yoke
> Of famine and disease that made
> A false necessity obeyed . .

And if Blake and Baudelaire were right to decry his neglect of the self, to predict that his dedication to "progress" would end in enslavement to the machine, Auden points out that it is to this dedication, fragmenting society and unsettling tradition, that we owe the truth once apparent only to the few, that "Aloneless is man's real condition," that each must send forth a questing Ego to seek his Way; we can no longer learn our good "From chances of a neighborhood/ Or class or party."

Ultimately, Auden locates the root of our troubles in the failure to do "Eros's legislative will." He explains that "The flood of tyranny and force/ Arises at a double source," and characteristically (one recalls the Lords of limit), he sees these as extremes towards which the devil tempts, involving a separating of the functions of ego and self. The first is "PLATO's lie of intellect," which locates truth in the abstractions of reason and makes it the concern of the elect; the other is "ROUSSEAU's falsehood of the flesh," which in contemporary form is Hitler's "metaphysics of the crowd," described in "Jacob and the Angel" as the "morbid abdication of the free-willing and individual before the collective and daemonic." And responsibility for both of these errors lies with the unwilling Ego, her refusal to use her freedom:

> . . . our political distress
> Descends from her self-consciousness,
> Her cold *concupiscence d'esprit*
> That looks upon her liberty
> Not as a gift from life with which
> To serve, enlighten, and enrich
> The total creature that could use
> Her function of free-will to choose
> The actions that this world requires
> To educate its blind desires,
> But as the right to lead alone
> An attic life all on her own . . .

Such things as Political Romanticism are a consequence of the Ego's despair at then finding its life deprived of necessity, for its response is "suicide," a romantically willed surrender to the furies of the neglected unconscious.

To define the proper relationship between ego and self Auden chooses an image of creative conflict, that of the wrestling bout. In prose echoing the lines quoted above, he declares that the liberals are wrong, reason is not self-sufficient, for we *are* lived by the daemon of the unconscious; but because the daemon cannot know its ends without an agent to discover them, it creates Jacob, "the prudent Ego":

> not for the latter to lead, in self-isolation and contempt, a frozen attic life of its own, but to be a loving and reverent antagonist; for it is only through that wrestling bout . . . that the future is born, that Jacob acquires the power and the will to live, and the demon is transformed into an angel.

Although the closing prayer of "New Year Letter" is distinctly Christian in its evocations, it seems to represent no commitment other than to this parable, retold in the note glossing the line ". . . the powers/ That we create with are not ours." If in some measure the prayer is to an orthodox God, probably, like most of Auden's prayers to this point, it has more in view the conception that "Man is aware that his actions do not express his real nature. God is a term for what he imagines that nature to be." In the phrase "My Father worketh and I work," Auden explains, " 'My Father' is the real nature of man; 'I' his conscious awareness of that nature."[18] "My Father" is the Logos implicit in the unconscious, "I" the ego that must seek, by employing its freedom, to make the Logos flesh.

The twenty "Quest" sonnets, in search of the Logos, invite us into a comic-surrealistic world of story book ordeals and desolate places, ogres and magical transformations, into the fun-house of the unconscious and its private perils, much in the manner of an effective source of imagery, *Alice in Wonderland* (if this had been written by Franz Kafka), or of Kafka himself, who, like Jung and Kierkegaard, is an obvious influence. Like "New Year Letter," "The Quest" is concerned with "the Way," but Auden's category is here "the Individual," and the most relevant commentary on the poems is Jung's remark that "A way is only *the* way when one finds it and follows it oneself."[19] Considered from an existential point of view, the Logos or "Necessary" which is object of the quest is inseparable from individuality, for each individual "The nature of Necessity like grief/ Exactly corresponding to his own." Informing this view is Kierkegaard's conception of truth as a subjective and inward relationship that the individual exists *in,* rather than as something knowable or known. Combining Kierkegaard and Jung, Auden sees this relationship as one with the unconscious, and, by placing the quest within a world of the pasteboard surreal—peopled with archetypes drawn from fairy tale and childhood dream—and by using images which metamorphose and disorient, he assimilates this view into his fable technique.

[18] "Christian on the Left," *Nation,* CXLIX (Sept. 1939), p. 273. The passage on the prudent Ego is from "Jacob and the Angel," p. 293.

[19] *The Integration of the Personality,* trans. Stanley Dell (London: Kegan Paul, Trench, Trubner & Co., 1949), p. 32. This book is an important influence on "New Year Letter" as well as on "The Quest."

In deference to the subjective nature of the Way, the sonnets deal mainly with the difficulties of properly setting out and with the temptations and misunderstandings leading one astray. They have little to say of success on the quest other than to indicate its inward character and its ultimate dependence upon sources outside the individual's control. Providing a glimpse into the garden which transforms existence, "The Door" suggests that success involves a coming into relation with the unconscious. "The Garden," however (St. Augustine's among others), reveals the important point that the relationship means not, in any normative sense, health, but the integration of personality described by Jung. Mocking the conventions of quest literature, "The Way" observes that no formula will guide us to this end, not even one derived from reversing customary practices. To support this point "The Lucky" and "The Hero" show that success depends on grace and virtues that may seem to others trivial. In "The Preparations," individuals are destroyed by their peculiar natures for regarding as an external matter something requiring a questioning of their natures, while "The City" reveals the danger of reaching a place where nature has been overcome (Cf. "The Capital"), so that moral freedom entails the danger of settling down to "being nobody." Those who arrive, in proper quest fashion, to seek their fortunes here find that the city offers not only what for them is the Necessary but also the freedom to disobey it; they fail the one requirement of the quest, which is that they become themselves. The three "Temptation" sonnets, exploring themes returned to in "The Sea and the Mirror," parallel Satan's testing of Christ. The first temptation is treated as the danger for the artist of using his magic so as to transform the frustrations of reality into fantasy satisfaction, the second as the surrender to nihilism threatening those impatient with the finitude of existence, the third as the temptation to yield for the sake of power to a cynicism distorting one's humanity.

Several of the remaining poems turn upon a distinction between the exceptional and the average, but this is to be understood not pejoratively, as in Jung, but with the humility of Kierkegaard's contention that the Knight of Faith may be unrecognizable, that, as Auden puts it, "Only God can tell the saintly from the suburban." Like both of these writers, Auden distinguishes between the true individual, conscious of his choices, and those for whom convention and conditioned response constitute all of self so that they have no being save in what Kierkegaard calls the "Crowd" or "the Public." To be exceptional enough to undertake the quest means simply to be reflective, however, and his concern in the poems is that this today is the position of each of us. "Today a man has only two choices," Auden writes: "he can be consciously passive or consciously active. He can accept deliberately or reject deliberately, but he must decide because his position in life is no longer a real necessity."[20] The Quest, then, is something we are all called upon, but for "The Average" the Way will lie in an acceptance of ordinary relationships, and the attempt to fill an exceptional role will frustrate self-realization. The point of "The Presumptuous" is that to be exceptional is to obey a call, what Jung calls a "vocation" and Kierkegaard "the voluntary"[21]—notions en-

[20] "Criticism in a Mass Society," in *The Intent of the Critic,* ed. Donald A. Stauffer (Princeton: Princeton University Press, 1941), p. 134. Auden writes in "The Wandering Jew" (*New Republic,* CIV, February 1941, p. 186): "To become exceptional— that is to say, to become reflective—is to discover that the Necessary itself, to the human vision, appears arbitrary."

[21] "A man cannot embark upon 'the voluntary' (the requirements of which are higher than the universal requirements) unless he has an *immediate certainty* that it is required of him *in particular.* From the point of view of the universal requirements, 'the voluntary' is in fact presumption . . . In order really to be a great genius, a man must be an exception. But in order that his being exceptional should be a serious matter he himself must be unfree, forced into the position. There lies the importance of his dementia. There is a definite point in which he suffers; it is impossible for him to run with the herd. Perhaps his dementia has nothing whatsoever to do with his real genius, but it is the pain by which he is nailed out in isolation—and he must be isolated if he is to be great; and no man can freely isolate himself; he must be com-

visioning the individual unfree to take a normal course, compelled out of the common way into a position conducive to his unique development. Those in the sonnet fail because, succumbing to the dangers of imitation, they choose a perilous course which for them is not compulsory.

If one recalls the old ideal of the "Truly Strong," this new notion of the exceptional will serve to underline the rejection of health as a criterion of value and help to explain why almost all the well-known figures in *Another Time* are carefully shown to have derived their creativity from abnormal circumstances. Pascal's view of man's destitute condition is traced to a lonely and loveless childhood; Matthew Arnold's moral denunciations are a servitude to his father and also an unconscious assault upon him; Edward Lear blossoms into nonsense by tapping the resources of his "Regret." These explanations are all baldly put forth and no doubt they oversimplify, but they reflect an interest in the circumstances from which unique accomplishments arise rather than an effort to explain away creative achievement by equating it with neurosis. In his own formulation of "the voluntary," Auden now writes, in an arresting statement, that "the true significance of a neurosis is teleological." He no longer means that it is a warning to change ways but, instead, that a child *seeks* a traumatic experience: "in order to find a necessity and direction for its existence, in order that its life may become a serious matter . . . a neurosis is a guardian angel; to become ill is to take vows."[22]

Despite an occasional use of Christian symbolism, "The Quest"

pelled if it is to be a serious matter." This passage from Kierkegaard's *Journals* is quoted in the "Notes" to *New Year Letter* (pp. 88-89).

"It is what is called vocation: an irrational factor that fatefully forces a man to emancipate himself from the herd and its trodden paths. True personality always has vocation and believes in it, has fidelity to it as to God . . . this vocation acts like a law of God from which there is no escape. That many go to ruin upon their own ways means nothing to him who has vocation. He must obey his own law, as if it were a demon that whisperingly indicated to him new and strange ways." This appears in Jung, *The Integration of the Personality,* p. 291.

22 "The Wandering Jew," p. 186.

reveals no unmistakable commitment to Christianity. The epilogue to *New Year Letter*, dated in *Collected Poetry* "Autumn 1940," is less ambiguous. Describing the reluctant return of the ego from sleep to the hostile, death-filled world in which choices are necessary, it raises a question at the heart of "The Quest" and upon which a purely "Ethical" view founders. In a world of war, with escape no more possible than indifference, how, willing though we may be, "can/ We will the knowledge that we must know to will?" The poem makes no answer but, as prerequisite to an answer, it asks us to acknowledge "One immortal, one infinite Substance" and "the Word which was/ From the beginning."

If we are not to misunderstand Auden's commitment to Christianity, we must grasp the point that the considerations finally impelling it were not intellectual ones. His personal experience, he tells us, was a genuine "conversion," something in which "suffering plays a greater part than knowledge." That our life is a gift, our powers not our own, he had always contended. From where one responds to this feeling by equating our powers with "love" and assigning one's awe to the unconscious, the way is not long, although it may be circuitous, to the conviction that existence stands in direct relationship to God—that our experience of dependence and obligation testifies that it is in God that our lives are grounded. Auden's acceptance of Christianity was an acceptance of self, an acknowledgment of feelings long present, which, as an "enlightened" mind, he had refused to express in an orthodox form—orthodoxy could too easily be seen as a rationalization: "Like so many of my generation who have been saved from many kinds of hypocrisy by the Freudian or Marxist premise that all thinking is 'interested' thinking, I forgot that this rule applies just as much to denying as it does to affirming."[23]

The personal experiences prompting conversion also, however,

[23] Auden, "Foreword" to Emile Cammaerts, *The Flower of Grass* (New York: Harper & Brothers, 1945), p. xii. For the comment on "conversion," see Howard Griffin, "Conversation on Cornelia Street: Dialogue with W. H. Auden," *Accent,* X (Autumn 1949), p. 52.

enforced a point that world conditions were suggesting independently and towards which his thought had been moving for some time. The same year *I Believe* was circulating his "fairly optimistic" opinion that badness in individuals was mainly the result of bad environment, Auden announced in a review the conviction that Democracy was hard, that it would only work "if as individuals we lead good lives." "I do not think that democracy can be sustained or defended," he argued, "unless one believes that pride, lying, and violence are mortal sins, and that their commission entails one's damnation."[24] This view is reflected in the insistence of "New Year Letter" that the devil can damn and that democracy begins with free confession of sin. But "sin" and "damnation" in what sense? And on what basis do we trust that the wrestling bout between ego and self will issue in law or equilibrium? As far as "reasons" ever motivate conversion, Auden's reason was that the failure to deal decisively with fascism short of war had shown that the liberal values so widely taken for granted were really dependent upon a sustaining foundation in Christianity. Why was it, he asks, that not only the Right but also the Left was deceived into thinking National Socialism in the interests of Capitalism? "Europe consented to Hitler," he answers, "because it had lost the sense of law which makes the recognition of an outlaw possible." Hitler carried to its logical conclusion every relativistic assumption of liberalism:

> He was neither understood nor resisted because millions of people had really accepted the same view of life, viz., that there is nothing which is unconditionally required, nothing for which one is in some sense or another eternally damned for doing or not doing, and therefore no reason for condemning or preventing the behavior of another unless it directly interferes with with [sic] oneself, that if one were Hitler in fact, one would do exactly the [same].[25]

[24] "Democracy is Hard," *Nation,* CXLIX (Oct. 1939), p. 386. Perhaps it is Democracy to which Poem XXIII from *Another Time* ("Not as that dream Napoleon") is addressed.

[25] "Where Are We Now," *Decision,* I (Jan. 1941), pp. 49-50, 51.

CHAPTER V

The Failure of Caliban and Ariel

THE SEA AND THE MIRROR—FOR THE TIME BEING—THE AGE OF ANXIETY

All chance, all love, all logic, you and I,
Exist by grace of the Absurd . . .
—"In Sickness and in Health"

IT would be a serious error to think of Auden's conversion as a surrender to the other-worldly, a disengagement from contemporary life and the earthly business of existence. The revitalization of theology that we have witnessed in our time, deriving largely from the writings of Søren Kierkegaard, has been distinctly existence-oriented. It began to attract Auden's interest shortly before the beginning of the war, and it is hard to imagine him, a persistent satirist of religious escapism in his early days, coming to Christianity by any other route. To be sure, Auden's is not a mind unresponsive to doctrine as such, but the point is that he has always assessed the validity of doctrine by reference to the existential predicament, the dilemma of being separated from self, and so separated from "law," by the fact of self-consciousness. In Kierkegaard, avidly read both before and after his conversion, he found a writer who put the question not, "What are the Christian truths?" but, "How is it possible to relate oneself to and be *in* the truth?"—and for whom this question was inseparable from another, that of how to become a self. Kierkegaard's answer—the definition of faith tirelessly repeated in the work with perhaps the most marked influence upon Auden of any in the Kierkegaardian canon, *The Sickness Unto Death*—was that "by relating itself to its own self and by willing to be itself the self is grounded transparently in the Power which posited it."[1] As a prescriptive statement, this is none too exact, but if we note the resemblance between this view of the self's relation to the source of its existence and Auden's own thinking on the subject of our relation to Eros, it will be clear that his conversion required no sharp severance from earlier habits of thought, no drastic change of orientation—only a sense of inner necessity and of religious faith as a personal reality.

"Where does the Logos come from?" Auden asks in 1940: "Is it an external gift of Grace or is it itself created by Eros?"[2] The Logos is the Necessary or Unconditional, the principle by which we are to love, and through "New Year Letter," although the situation is somewhat changed when we reach "The Quest," his answer had been that the Logos is Eros fulfilled, fulfillment being the wrestling into fact of "Natural Law." The change apparent in "The Quest" is that now the standpoint from which Natural Law is regarded is not human nature, but the unique nature of the individual. The contribution here of the Kierkegaardian view of faith is to dissolve the sense of sharp alternatives between what we are in ourselves and what seems willed for us by a higher authority. If the Logos is the word of God, then in a real sense we achieve it, as it seems often in experience, even to the secular-minded, by a gift of Grace; but if God is the power positing us, the subjective ground of our being, faith is not a commitment to something beyond the world but a way of living—by choosing to be oneself—and the Logos is not a principle imposed from without but the very substance of self-fulfillment. In Kierkegaard's treatment of faith, Auden found his elusive conception of natural law transformed into the will of God and placed beyond the bounds of empirical criticism by an insistence upon subjectivity; and in subjec-

[1] *Fear and Trembling and The Sickness Unto Death,* trans. Walter Lowrie (Garden City, New York: Doubleday, 1954), p. 147 and elsewhere.

[2] "A Literary Transference," *Southern Review,* VI (Summer 1956), p. 84.

tivity he discovered a means by which faith could be seen as inseparable from self-fulfillment. The Necessary is not on the order of a biological drive given within us, nor is it something we must or can, in the objective sense, know; it is what we are when, in faith, we choose to be ourselves.

It would be misleading, though, to think of Auden's understanding of his own conversion and of the Christian view of existence, particularly with regard to the question of subjectivity, as that of a thorough-going Kierkegaardian. Certainly in Kierkegaard's conception of Christianity as an acceptance of the Absurd and in his insistence upon our paradoxical obligation to become that which in fact we are, Auden discovered illuminations that were to become central to his own thinking. After this, his indebtedness to Kierkegaard, like his indebtedness to many writers, consists in the borrowing of categories of thought to be used for a diversity of purposes and shaped to the needs of the occasion. Thus, we shall find exploited Kierkegaard's conception of the "Crowd" and the "Public," of "despair" and the "leap" of faith by which despair is conquered, and, perhaps most conspicuously of all, his notion of the three stages of the Aesthetic, the Ethical, and the Religious—which furnished an organizing schemework that could be used in poetry. Perhaps, too, Auden's practice of the art of parable, often in reliance upon this schemework, owes something to the example of Kierkegaard, who, in *Either/Or*, applies this mode of analysis to figures who have engaged Auden's own attention (e.g., Don Juan). Particularly the three stages, however, Auden alters to his own way of thinking, and reveals thereby its divergence from Kierkegaard's. In an essay on his conversion, he observes that one of Kierkegaard's talents was to make Christianity sound bohemian, but he feels compelled to add the criticism that one can read through Kierkegaard's entire works and find little hint that life is lived with the body.[3]

In an important sense, Auden's outlook has more in common

3 *Modern Canterbury Pilgrims,* ed. James A. Pike (New York: Morehouse-Gorham, 1956), p. 42.

with the views of Reinhold Niebuhr, who takes the Kierkegaardian conception of the human situation as a synthesis of finitude and freedom, necessity and possibility, and in line with Auden's own tendencies conducts his analysis within the framework of divided consciousness and an unKierkegaardian respect for our creaturely as well as our spiritual endowment. Because to Niebuhr the temptation to sin is the anxiety resulting from man's simultaneous involvement in and capacity to transcend nature—the anxiety personified by Auden as the devil—sin resides chiefly in the effort to dissociate oneself from either self or ego:

> Man is insecure and involved in natural contingency; he seeks to overcome his insecurity by a will-to-power which overreaches the limits of human creatureliness. Man is ignorant and involved in the limitations of a finite mind; but he pretends that he is not limited. He assumes that he can gradually transcend finite limitations . . .
>
> Sometimes man seeks to solve the problem of the contradiction of finiteness and freedom, not by seeking to hide his finiteness and comprehending the world into himself, but by seeking to hide his freedom and by losing himself in some aspect of the world's vitalities. In that case his sin may be defined as sensuality rather than pride. Sensuality is never the mere expression of natural impulse in man. It always betrays some aspect of his abortive effort to solve the problem of finiteness and freedom.[4]

The implied insistence here on synthesis, on the flesh and its contingencies as well as on the spirit, coupled—perhaps paradoxically—with an attention steadily focussed on the distinction between flesh and spirit, constitutes an important respect in which both Niebuhr and Auden differ from Kierkegaard despite their indebtedness to him.

In early Auden, such a synthesis seems to entail little more than a dethronement and assimilation of the ego by the self, a sweeping

[4] *The Nature and Destiny of Man* (London: James Nisbet, 1941), I, pp. 190-91.

of the insensitive refuse from the burning core. No doubt, Auden, like Lawrence too at his best, would have granted that the enemy was not mind in itself but only its wrong employment, its defence of "old systems" imposed from without and frustrating our inner needs, would have conceded that, when exercised to serve these deeper tendencies, the ego had its indispensable function. The warning against opposite extremes which John Blair cites as a characteristic Auden strategy—and which emerges from Auden's recognition of the perils of divided consciousness—appears early in his work. Even while acknowledging the unconscious as the nourisher of life and warning that the "fate of the insolent mind that takes/ Truth as itself is homicidal phantasies . . . aphasia and general paralysis of the insane," he hastens to add that "by opposite error also is man deceived/ Seeking a heaven on earth he chases his shadow." Nevertheless, the emphasis of the early work is preponderantly one-sided and the role accorded the ego is minimal. It is an emphasis enforced by style, one which eschews the precise articulations of intellect, which often suggests the voice of the prophet speaking in obedience, or in tight-lipped deference, to an overmastering fate. Only at the close of "Journal of an Airman" is self-consciousness clearly acknowledged an asset, "in fact the only friend of our progress," and it is not until the "In Time of War" sonnets that freedom is convincingly seen as intrinsically precious and as necessary to self-fulfillment as necessity, rather than as a corrective to be exercised while Eros recuperates. At this point, ego and self emerge as partners in a wrestling bout, with victory possible only so long as neither party is defeated.

If for Auden as a Christian, this conception retains its validity, self-fulfillment in its highest form now implies *agape*, that love for others defined in the astounding injunction dulled for us by familiarity, that we are to love our neighbors as we love ourselves—which is to say, unconditionally. This may seem an ideal excessively deprivatory to the self, but it should be observed that Auden's respect for the finite and the creaturely operates in the insistence that the works of love are done with the body and require an acceptance of the here and now, and that self-fulfillment is synonymous with *agape* only when we have reached that point in our own development where a full acceptance of others is self-fulfilling; for Auden has not become a preacher of pieties, unaware that the saintly life requires vocation and the aid of Grace. Our human obligation is to be true to ourselves; there are few so aware that the danger of presumption may be to meet the ogre and be turned to stone.

The three long works of the 1940's, still defined by the search for the "Way," are not yet the works of Auden as Christian, but of Auden as convert. Centered around the existential wrestling bout, the creative conflict between ego and self shaping authentic existence, they locate the "Natural" way in the "Kingdom of Anxiety" and find that the temptation to "idolatry," to escape the problem of finiteness and freedom by recourse to what is, in essence, the familiar dualism of the devil, can be conquered only by religious faith. Faith requires a leap in the dark, and particularly Christian faith, which from the rational viewpoint is utterly absurd. One of Auden's main points, and it lies at the heart of "The Sea and the Mirror," is that human resources must first be found inadequate, that the leap will not take place until, having confronted our predicament, we find the darkness visible.

"The Sea and the Mirror" is a loose allegory, a reading of *The Tempest* as existential parable, accomplished by a lifting of Shakespeare's curtain to recall each of the characters for a final speech and by an expansion of the original epilogue, asking the audience for a show of applause, into a lengthy commentary on the relationship, not really between life and art, but between the actual and the imagined, that which receives form and that which supplies it—between "what is" as opposed to "what is possible." It may be gathered that divided consciousness is not only a deliberate theme here but a structuring principle. These oppositions are functions of the distinction between self and ego; they are embodied as

Caliban and Ariel, and appear in the poem's major symbols of sea and mirror and also sea and desert—conflicting principles which be reconciled.

In fact, the poem accomplishes no such reconciliation. In the concluding section, spoken by a Caliban triumphantly gifted with the fastidious and elaborate late prose manner of Henry James, "The Sea and the Mirror" achieves the rare privilege of becoming conscious of itself, and particularly of its reception by ourselves, its audience; so that deprived of a disinterested vantage point outside the poem, and suddenly having become its subject matter, we are placed in the position of having to achieve the reconciliation in our own lives, with the show over—of being unable to applaud. This situation reflects Auden's conception of the true function of art; both mimetic and paradigmatic, its purpose is not only to show us as we truly are but also, by its example of order, to suggest that we might be different and better. Its proper effect is "disenchanting":

> By significant details, it shows us that our present state is neither as virtuous nor as secure as we thought, and by the lucid pattern into which it unifies these details, its assertion that order is possible, it faces us with the command to make it *actual*.[5]

Seeing ourselves as we really are, we may hear for the first time, Auden suggests, the "real Word which is our only *raison d'etre*," and which is the basis of faith and of the order which art symbolizes. In its "feebly figurative" way, art provides a glimpse of ultimate reconciliation, of the garden in the desert, the island in the sea by which the Absurd is vindicated; but granted a glimpse of possible order, we cannot rest content; we must exert our efforts to make it actual.

It is Prospero's problem, of course, to have failed this obligation; and as the poem opens we see the aged magician severing

5 "The Poet of the Encirclement," *New Republic,* CIX (Oct. 1943), p. 579.

his ties with Ariel and happy to be leaving his enchanted island. In a brilliant essay on the master-servant relationship in literature called "Balaam and His Ass," Auden observes that "both the repentance of the guilty and the pardon of the injured seem more formal than real" in *The Tempest*, and that Prospero, though not without admirable qualities, "has the coldness of someone who has come to the conclusion that human nature is not worth much," without realizing that he, too, "might have erred and be in need of pardon."[6] Auden's Prospero, though he retains his skepticism and coldness, has achieved this realization and come to recognize the misuse of his art. Thanks to Ariel, he concedes, the "lonely and unhappy are very much alive," for reality need not be faced when Ariel is around to console or beguile us; it can be a springboard for imagination, a stimulus whose only meaning is our own response. But Prospero now knows Ariel's true function as the "spirit of reflection"—it is to provide a mirror from which "All we are not stares back at what we are"; and that for himself art had been the opposite of disenchanting: "the power to enchant/ That comes from disillusion." Auden has always acknowledged the Freudian view that art may arise from an effort to escape from reality into a realm offering compensation for personal limitations. For Prospero, who "tempted Antonio into treason," art was a means of triumphantly asserting himself against conditions of reality he could not accept:

> When I woke into my life, a sobbing dwarf
> Whom giants served only as they pleased, I was not what
> I seemed;
> Beyond their busy backs I made a magic
> To ride away from a father's imperfect justice,
> Take vengeance on the Romans for their grammar,
> Usurp the popular earth and blot out for ever
> The gross insult of being a mere one among many . . .[7]

[6] "Balaam and His Ass," *The Dyer's Hand* (New York: Random House, 1962), pp. 128-29. This essay originally appeared in 1954.

[7] "The Sea and the Mirror" and "For the Time Being" originally

A peculiar blend of thankfulness and wry discernment, Prospero's speech expresses a wisdom born from the cynicism of self-knowledge. With age he has come to see that in life's bargains one gets away with nothing, that Ariel's tricks are really a species of test, and that despite his wish for detachment, he has exacted of Caliban "absolute devotion" and broken the promise he made as an apprentice. He is skeptical of others because he now realizes the price he has paid for his art and the difficulties he will face without it. Only now, having released Ariel, can Prospero believe that he must suffer and die, that up until now he has failed to live:

> . . . as if through the ages I had dreamed
> About some tremendous journey I was taking,
> Sketching imaginary landscapes, chasms and cities,
> . . . .
> And now, in my old age, I wake, and this journey really exists,
> And I have actually to take it . . .

All this has a meaning satisfactory enough on the literal level of events—literal, given the poem's particular setting and fantasy elements, its transparent identification of magic with art. With the aid of Ariel, Prospero has exercised his "gift/ In dealing with shadows" to evade coming to grips with his human and mortal nature. Awakened to his delinquency by the intrusion on his island, he recognizes the tyrant's use that he has made of Caliban and is preparing to return to the world, to face the limitations of being himself and bear the sufferings he had tried to avoid. There are, however, further reaches of meaning in this particular aspect of *The Tempest*, interpreted as a parable of artistic detachment. We shall be in a position to appreciate them once we realize that Auden's allegory is loose, not in the sense that its symbols are contradictory or vague—they are strikingly exact—but only in its com-

---

appeared in *For the Time Being* (New York: Random House, 1944; London: Faber and Faber, 1945). Quotations in this chapter are from the American edition of *The Collected Poetry of W. H. Auden* (New York: Random House, 1945; London: Faber and Faber, 1948).

mitment to horizontal development. Anticipating an allegory geared to incident, we soon find ourselves up against major incongruities: Since Ariel is surely Imagination, how can he cease to accompany Prospero? If the sea is life, what will be Prospero's position when, having crossed the sea, he is home in Milan? Questions such as these, predicated on the assumption that allegory is a sort of shadow cast by the story line, ignore the fact that many allegories (Conrad's "The Secret Sharer" would be an example) are situational rather than sequential, and operate not to supply an additional narrative horizontal beneath the literal one, but to superimpose upon this a vertical perspective of extended meaning. Auden accomplishes this aim by means of allegorical images which reveal a fixed dimension of implication only when we suspend the tyranny of the story line and establish their significance within a key situation.

In the present case, the governing situation is Prospero's relation to his enchanted island. This, of course, is the domain of his art, and Prospero's problem is that he has lived here, has sought it as a refuge, and so failed to live in reality. Within this situation Ariel, we can see, is Imagination, and the sea is life, or reality itself, the element from which Prospero has been isolated but into which he has now thrown his books and upon which he is about to voyage. Auden's study of Romantic symbolism, *The Enchafèd Flood*, tells us that the "sea or the great waters . . . are the symbol for the primordial undifferentiated flux, the substance which became created nature only by having form imposed upon or wedded to it."[8] From the standpoint of the individual, this is the task of self-definition, requiring self-acceptance[9] and the faith that Prospero, "an old man/ Just like other old men," is now acquiring. To

[8] *The Enchafèd Flood* (London: Faber and Faber, 1951), p. 18.

[9] According to Kierkegaard, the "poet-existence," from a Christian standpoint, is sin—"the sin of poetizing instead of being, of standing in relation to the Good and the True through imagination instead of being that, or rather existentially striving to be it." (*The Sickness Unto Death*, p. 208.)

Kierkegaard, the situation of faith is to be "Sailing alone, out over seventy thousand fathoms." Borrowing these words, Auden indicates that in its ultimate significance the element Prospero must face is the "Absurd"; the sea is the apparent meaninglessness of existence upon which the voyage of faith must be risked.

As "Balaam and His Ass" explains, an important literary use of the master-servant relationship is to express symbolically the "inner dialogue of human personality." We have already identified Ariel with Imagination, the means by which the artist works his magic, and it has been suggested often enough in Shakespearian criticism that Caliban is "natural man," an incarnation of our creaturely heritage symbolically parallel to the sea and requiring, to be truly human, the taking on of form. If we recognize that Caliban and Ariel are Prospero's servants, embodying two facets of a single personality of which Prospero himself represents a third, we shall have a further perspective from which to view him. Offering a hypothetical example of psychic dialogue, Auden enumerates five participants: Self, Cognitive Ego, Super-Ego, Volitional Ego, Body. He observes that only one,

> my cognitive ego, really employs the indicative mood. Of the others, my self and my super-ego cannot, either of them, be a servant. Each is a master who is either obeyed or disobeyed. Neither can take orders. My body, on the other hand . . . can do nothing but what it is told; it can never be a master, nor even a servant, only a slave. While my volitional ego is always both, a servant in relation to either my self or my super-ego and a master in relation to my body.[10]

"The Sea and the Mirror" utilizes a much simpler and foreshortened arrangement, but it will be helpful to see how the two coincide. As Imagination, Ariel is the Cognitive Ego, though viewed in a special capacity, as reporter not of the real, but of the possible. Elsewhere in the essay, Auden observes that imagination

10 "Balaam and His Ass," p. 112.

is "without desire and is, therefore, incapable of distinguishing between permitted and forbidden possibilities." For this reason it employs the indicative mood, for it can only be a servant: the business of actualizing possibility belongs elsewhere. It belongs, specifically, to the Volitional Ego, and this is represented by Prospero, whose failing has been to evade his task, to have wandered in the possible so as to avoid the obligation to make the possible real. As a young man, Prospero vowed "To hate nothing and to ask nothing for its love"—he tried not to exist at all, by dissociating himself from the needs and limitations of his creaturely nature. This nature is, of course, embodied in Caliban, not only the Body but also the Self, which is why, although a slave, he appears monstrous and has grown rebellious; for the self, with wishes of its own to express, has been asked for absolute devotion. It will be noticed that the Super-Ego has not been accounted for. Its role is filled by the existential imperative which informs the poem: "To thine own self be true." This means, referring back to the Kierkegaardian dictum, that by an act of faith, the ego must relate itself to the self, and choose as an actual self the self made possible by self-acceptance. If Prospero is will, Ariel is the ego and Caliban the self who have been kept from relationship by a will in despair.

A portrait of the artist as a wry and mocking commentator on life become aware of the consequences of his detachment, the Prospero section serves to introduce major symbols and associations (the "Journey of Life" and the relationship of Ariel to solipsism being two not yet mentioned) and to embody theme on the level of recognizable personality. It is only in the third section that many of the allegorical suggestions we have noted are elaborated and given retrospective significance. In one passage, Caliban is designated "no less a person than the nude august elated archer of our heaven, the darling single son of . . . our great white Queen of Love herself," and in another, warning again that the artist may give himself so entirely to art as to neglect to live, he is established as the demon Jacob must transform into an angel:

> Had you tried to destroy me, had we wrestled through long dark hours, we might by daybreak have learnt something from each other; in some panting pause to recover breath for further more savage blows or in the moment before your death or mine, we might both have heard together that music which explains and pardons all.

Caliban, then, is Eros, the raw energy of love which we must set in order as we struggle to become ourselves, and music, an example of the order of art, is here the sign of Grace. If Auden's tone while locating his god in the pantheon is somewhat mocking, this reflects the discrepancy between art and life: measured against the world of art (as he is in this section), the offspring of the Queen of Love can only appear the disruptive son of the witch Chaos.

Part II is entitled "The Supporting Cast" and then "Sotto Voce," and whether this addition was meant as a comment or merely as an indication that each character speaks in private, this section, because it provides for even the minor characters, reveals a certain slackening of thematic tensions. Almost all the speeches do disclose, though, the loneliness of the existential situation, and most have a closer relation than is immediately evident to the analysis of this situation as it strains between the poles of divided consciousness, the transcendental and the creaturely, in accord with the revelatory experience made possible by Prospero's art. The songs of Ferdinand and Miranda are complementary: awakened from a mirror world of storybook imaginings, she rejoices to have found her Prince Charming in the flesh, while he exults in a love that will be completed in the flesh because of his new awareness of a spiritual dimension. Adrian and Francisco had scoffed at Gonzalo's intuition of miraculous order; now, goldfish become "Good little sunbeams" (just as Caliban's element is the sea, Ariel's is air) and knowing better, they must learn to aspire. Similarly, in Stephano's speech, the contrast is between an ambition of mind (Stephano's drunken wish to be the god Caliban had taken him for) and the waywardness of the flesh. Stephano's predicament is the human predicament: "Between the bottle and the 'loo'/ A lost thing looks for a lost name."

The speeches of the remaining characters, although Antonio is a special case, all bear upon the theme of faith versus despair[11] and show the extent to which each has been aided on the island to become himself in face of the temptation to exaggerate the claims of one dimension of being. Gonzalo alone had noticed the special properties of the magic island, realizing that the miraculous escape, the clothes which seemed new-dyed, bespoke an order of existence out of the ordinary. But the officiousness causing the rejection of his consolations, the grandiloquent theorizings into which he converted his experience, convict the old counsellor of "Doubt and insufficient love":

> There was nothing to explain:
> Had I trusted the Absurd
> And straightforward note by note
> Sung exactly what I heard,
> Such immediate delight
> Would have taken there and then
> Our common welkin by surprise,
> All would have begun to dance
> Jigs of self-deliverance.

[11] This may be said of Trinculo and the Master and Boatswain as well, although such a view probably imposes a heavier weight of interpretation than their speeches call for. Trinculo has discovered that he is in despair—which is to say, that his existence bears little relationship to his real self; while the Master and Boatswain evidence what Kierkegaard describes as "The Despair which is Unconscious that it is Despair, or the Despairing Unconsciousness of having a Self and an Eternal Self." Kierkegaard says of the individual who suffers in this way that "the sensuous nature and the psycho-sensuous completely dominate him; the reason is that he lives in the sensuous categories agreeable/disagreeable, and says goodbye to truth, etc.; the reason is that he is too sensuous to have the courage to venture to be spirit or to endure it." (*The Sickness Unto Death,* p. 176.) Interestingly, the Master and Boatswain are the only characters not shown to have landed on the enchanted island.

Whereas Prospero's failure of faith had taken the form of substituting fantasy for reality, Gonzalo had turned from the evidence of his senses to the gropings of intellect, from incarnate order to the *idea* of an ideal commonwealth. For Gonzalo, the confirmation of his vision is healing and restores "subjective passion."

Two remarks by Prospero offer aid with Sebastian's difficult sestina, his reference to the journey he had taken only as a dream and his comparison of childhood and age. Auden observes in "Mundus et Infans" that the infant is "A pantheist not a solipsist," but this is not true of the *child*, who has achieved a sense of himself:

> The child runs out to play in the garden, convinced
> That the furniture will go on with its thinking lesson,
> Who, fifty years later, if he plays at all,
> Will first ask its kind permission to be excused.

The child is a solipsist not in the sense that he believes himself the only existence (it is the adult who fears for the existence of the kitchen table if he averts his mind from the factual) but in that, failing to distinguish what is pretended from what is, he inhabits a dreamlike world where "all wishes wear a crown/ And anything pretended is alive." Describing the "breaking of the childish spell," Caliban acknowledges that Ariel is the presiding genius of childhood:

> . . . so long as it enclosed you, there was, for you, no miracle, no magic, for everything that happened was a miracle—it was just as extraordinary for a chair to be a chair as for it to turn into a horse; it was no more absurd that the girding on of coalscuttle and poker should transform you into noble Hector than that you should have a father and mother who called you Tommy—and it was therefore only necessary for you to presuppose one genius, one unrivalled I to wish these wonders in all their endless plenitude and novelty to be . . .

But to awake from the dream, Caliban continues, is to "reckon with the two of us . . . to detect the irreconcilable difference between my reiterated affirmation of what your furnished circumstances categorically are, and His [i.e., Ariel's] successive propositions as to everything else which they conditionally might be." With the aid of these observations, we can see that Sebastian has undergone just such an awakening. He is one for whom the solipsism of childhood had become the nihilism of the conscienceless; for the "lie of Nothing" is the delusion that wishes are as real as fact, that nothing is but thinking makes it so. Provided with the opportunity to gain a kingdom, Sebastian found it easy to believe Alonso "was a dream/ I should not love because I had no proof." For this reason, the failure of his conspiracy has been salutary:

> My rioters all disappear, my dream
> Where Prudence flirted with a naked sword,
> Securely vicious, crumbles; it is day;
> Nothing has happened; we are all alive:
> I am Sebastian, wicked still, my proof
> Of mercy that I wake without a crown.

Because it provides a clash with inviolable substance, failure exposes the dreamer to the force of his delusion; for Sebastian it brings a sense of his own existence and of the reality, not of what might be, but of fact and of the present.

As for Alonso himself, he had aided in originally deposing Prospero, but now, "having heard the solemn/ Music strike" and suffered his sea-change, he steps forward as Auden's image of the Good King, concerned to impress upon his son the proper attitude toward power and a respect for the claims to be balanced if he would rule the Just City. Symbolically embodying these claims are the sea and the desert, the undisciplined but vital energies of existence as opposed to the ordered but arid contours of abstract form; they provide a structure of polarities ultimately reconciled by the image of the "spring in the desert, the fruitful/ Island in the sea"; but they only gradually reveal their root significance, and only as concentric layers of association are stripped away. Auden's comments in *The Enchafèd Flood* are very relevant. He points out that both the sea and the desert are the "wilderness, i.e., the place where there is no community, just or unjust, and no historical change for better or for worse" (p. 25). Alonso's evocation as the poem begins of the sea's indifference to the royal prerogative and of the desert's indiscriminateness as a dumping-ground serves as a warning that the proper exercise of human authority rests upon a respect for its communal foundations and upon an awareness of its finite and transitory nature.

One may go too far, perhaps, in attempting to find consistent interconnections between Auden's symbols as projections, ultimately, of matter and mind; but into this duality they finally resolve, and his schematic bent and approval of riddle as an element in poetry do not discourage the effort. The limitations of authority (the crown) and of its constituted power (the sceptre) continue as theme as we move into the poem, but if desert and sea, each appropriately menacing, still have the significance of provinces outside the ruler's control, we may note that "ocean flats where no subscription/ Concerts are given" suggests the slowness of matter in aspiring to form, while the desert plain where there is nothing to eat indicates the remoteness from reality of utopian ambitions. Two temptations arise for the prince: rather than balancing wishes with fact, he may turn tyrant, and drown in his animal energies, or turn recluse, to face the multitude's contempt and contend with disembodied terrors. Since the prince's own temperament determines the danger, only self-knowledge will reveal to Ferdinand which he has more to fear, the efreet offering an illusory liberation from the finitude of matter, or the siren who soothes the flesh by dulling the mind; the point of the poem is that "The Way of Justice is a tightrope."

In the City itself, where the aim is to combine both "civil pattern and importance," the alternative dangers are sterile regimentation (the "triviality of the sand") and meaningless turmoil ("watery vagueness"), and an extreme reaction to one or the other state can quickly bring on either the fire or the ice by which societies are destroyed. As ruler, Ferdinand is advised that he must look upon failure as a means of correction, that as a discipline for disorderly energies or as a release from enervating pride, it may lead to the "spring in the desert, the fruitful/ Island in the sea." *The Enchafèd Flood* tells us that the oasis or happy island (they are no different from the garden of "New Year Letter") represents "the earthly paradise where there is no conflict between natural desire and moral duty" (p. 29); it is the state of integration "where flesh and mind/ Are delivered from mistrust," and an image, too, of the perspective of faith from which Alonso speaks.

All the speeches we have examined, each in its own verse form, may be taken to contribute a chord to the music of reconciliation with which *The Tempest* ends. To the extent that there is drama in this section, it is provided by Antonio, who has been totally unmoved by Prospero's arrangement of a happy ending. Prospero believes that since both were in the wrong, forgiveness is mutual; but in Shakespeare's closing scene, Antonio utters no word to indicate he has reformed, and to the contributions of each of the other characters Auden adds a discordant note by Antonio of independence and defiance:

> *Your all is partial, Prospero;*
> *My will is all my own:*
> *Your need to love shall never know*
> *Me: I am I, Antonio,*
> *By choice myself alone.*

Predicating his existence on the urge to deny his brother peace, Antonio exemplifies Kierkegaard's conception of "defiant despair." Despair for Kierkegaard usually entails an alienation from one's authentic self; it is the state of being unconscious of this self, or, as in Prospero's case, of refusing to accept the self. But defiant despair is different; it is the "despair of willing despairingly to be oneself":

> . . . with hatred for existence it wills to be itself, to be itself in terms of its misery; it does not even in defiance or defiantly will to be itself, but to be itself in spite; it does not even will in defiance to tear itself free from the Power which posited it, it wills to obtrude upon this Power in spite, to hold on to it out of malice . . . it thinks it has hold of a proof against it, against its goodness. This proof the despairer thinks he himself is, and that is what he wills to be, therefore he wills to be himself . . .[12]

Regarding himself as living refutation of the principle of order revealed through Prospero's art, Antonio, from Prospero's point of view, represents the uncontrollable element in existence which frustrates our wishes. He must be for Prospero a constant source of temptation, for so long as he exists the urge will be present to don again the magician's robes and solve by an escape into art the problems which defy solution in life. But it is possible to regard these considerations from a somewhat different angle. As Prospero's brother, Antonio may be seen as simply an aspect of Prospero himself, his worse self, so to speak, or fallen will. In this light, it is significant that when Prospero abdicated power, Antonio ruled in Milan. Once again the major threat to Prospero's faith will be his own tendency to give way to despair.

The Tempest ends in reconciliation. We may suspect with Auden an undiminished recalcitrance in Antonio, but the scene before our eyes is one of concord—or almost so, for what of Caliban? About Ariel we are not overly troubled; we know he has won his freedom, and it is easy enough to imagine him dissolving into air; but Caliban is to be left behind on the island, the one incongruous element in an otherwise harmonious picture, as if he existed outside the world whose order is shared by the other char-

[12] *The Sickness Unto Death,* p. 207.

acters. The English Muse is a genial society hostess, Auden points out, a mixer of the genres not too concerned about "what the strait-laced Unities might possibly think or sad sour Probability possibly say," but Caliban seems alien to her amenable gatherings, the "solitary exception" she is never at home to. The final section is concerned with the riddle of Caliban as he appears to the audience. Shakespeare's epilogue had contained the request: "As you from crimes would pardon'd be/ Let your indulgence set me free." Auden's reveals an audience much too unsettled by an affront to propriety to grant this plea.

Sensing in Caliban "the represented principle of *not* sympathizing, *not* associating, *not* amusing," the audience call for an explanation, only to find themselves confronted, since Caliban is speaking their thoughts, with the "begged question" they would like explained. The suggestion is that they have been brought face to face with reality, but, as we have seen, Caliban is not exactly reality, which can be ordered by art, but the stuff of which reality, and selfhood, is made, and which requires in the making a responsible agent. Expecting a final curtain to pack away the show and clear the stage, and finding themselves, instead, staring at Caliban, the audience are in the position of the child who has awakened from the solipsistic dream; their clamor signifies a disturbing and unwelcome sense of task. If life, as Caliban suggests, is a journey, they, or (perhaps, better) we, have been brought to the "main depot, the Grandly Average Place," which is the realization that the journey exists and is ours to undertake. Auden suggests that it is possible we will get no farther, because a choice of destination requires faith. The "three or four decisive instants of transportation" open to us are life-changing decisions, Kierkegaardian "leaps." It is likely that, instead of taking them so as to arrive at selfhood, we will put our trust in either Caliban or Ariel and despair.

Auden's comments in two essays are extremely helpful here. In one, a review of Denis de Rougemont's *Love in the Western World*, he explains that "The task of the human Eros is how to actualize the possible by a series of decisions in which one future possibility is grasped by the present, and the rest thereby rendered impossible." Owing to the uncertainty of our condition, this is not so easy as it sounds:

> . . . to be aware that more than one possibility exists is to be aware that it is possible to make the wrong decision, that self-actualization is only achieved if the right decision is taken, and that if any of the wrong decisions are taken, the result will be self-negation. The human Eros is thus placed in a "catastrophic situation" to avoid the reality of which it tends to flee in two directions. Either it hides from the possible and attempts to live, like the animals, only in the actual . . .
>
> Or, alternatively, man's Eros can hide from the actual and attempt to live only in the possible . . .[13]

In the second essay, entitled "A Preface to Kierkegaard," the same point is formulated by reference to the Kierkegaardian categories. Lacking faith, Auden suggests, the individual must either despair or (what amounts in the end to the same thing) become an "idolater" and "invent an illusion of absolute certainty out of the individual passion of his immediate moods (the Esthetic) or the universal abstractions of his intellect (the Ethical)."[14] As we shall have occasion to observe again, this view of the categories is not wholly accurate, since to Kierkegaard the Ethical implies not merely an intellectual awareness of universal principles (which would be an Aesthetic awareness) but living commitment. However, it is significant that in his reading of Kierkegaard Auden should maintain the primacy of his habitual framework and insist on the distinction between ego and self. It is a way, even when

[13] "Eros and Agape," *Nation,* CLII (June 1941), p. 757.

[14] "A Preface to Kierkegaard," *New Republic,* CX (May 1944), p. 683. In this same essay, Auden defines despair as an inability to act, but this is not a conception elsewhere evident in his work, although an inability to act *authentically* would be despair in Kierkegaard's usage. Auden does not seem to use the term in a specialized sense.

picturing the dangers of separation, of stressing their distinctive and equally valid claims.

To turn to Caliban, then, would be to attempt to give oneself up to things as they are, to immerse oneself in the innocent delights of pure sense experience so as to escape the responsibility which comes with self-awareness.[15] Specifically, it is an effort to surrender reflection, to flee from ideas, discipline, and any formulation or awareness of the possible in the hope of gaining release from anxiety and the lost security erroneously associated with childhood. The problem is that Caliban's world is not, as imagination pictures it, Eden, but a bleak domain of primary qualities and geometrical shapes, where nature means scientific necessity, so that "all events are tautological repetitions and no decision will ever alter the secular stagnation." Lacking possibility and any suggestion of relationship, it is a world "with nowhere to go on to," the "ultimately liberal condition" where whatever is, is. Only in the sense that he can now envision no other is the individual able here to be himself—his existence "free at last to choose its own meaning, that is, to plunge headlong into despair and fall through silence fathomless and dry, all fact your single drop, all value your pure alas."

For the more capable minority who turn to Ariel, despair is equally unavoidable, though it takes a different form. They are those who have been granted what Auden calls "ethical authority"[16] but who react from their privileged glimpse of order into a disdain for the messiness of "particularized life." In contrast to

[15] "Give me my passage home, let me see that harbour once again just as it was before I learned the bad words." In "Balaam and His Ass" (p. 130), Auden points out that, owing to Prospero, Caliban "has lost his savage innocence," and he quotes from *The Tempest:* "You taught me language and my profit on't/ Is, I know how to curse." He also says that in a stage production of the play, Caliban should suggest, "as far as decency permits, the phallic." Attentive readers will note that at one point he follows this suggestion himself.

[16] See *The Enchafèd Flood,* pp. 84-86.

their earthy counterparts, their wish is not to be spared the burden of spiritual responsibility but the contingencies of material existence, "to transcend *any* condition" by escaping from the concreteness of the here and now to the "Heaven of the Really General Case." Shunning commitment to fact and to the present, they inhabit a sphere of pure possibility in which imagination encompasses "All the phenomena of an empirically ordinary world," but only as forms, so that there is no way of relating appearance to reality, no point of reference for gauging the import of events, no "knowledge of where on earth one has come from or where on earth one is going to." For followers of Ariel, only physical pain has unequivocal meaning, for, in Kierkegaard's words, the despair of the man who refuses to submit to the necessary in himself is that he does not "become aware of himself, aware that the self he is, is a perfectly definite something."[17]

In picturing the alternative routes to despair, Auden's point, of course, is that a meaningful existence requires both freedom and necessity, that ego and self are mutually interdependent—the point of the "Postscript," where Ariel sings to Caliban and the prompter's echoing "I" is an augur of integration. It is a point we have come to expect, but it is important to see that it rests in "The Sea and the Mirror" upon a basis different from that of "New Year Letter," with its comparable warning against Rousseau's "falsehood of the flesh" and Plato's "lie of intellect" and its declared faith in natural law. Shortly after the publication of the earlier poem, reviewing Reinhold Niebuhr's *The Nature and Destiny of Man,* Auden confesses that he finds the theory of natural law "ultimately untenable."[18] According to Niebuhr, the theory rests upon

[17] *The Sickness Unto Death,* p. 169.

[18] "The Means of Grace," *New Republic,* CIV (June 1941), p. 766. The same year, he announces the view that "Man is a fallen creature with a natural bias to do evil"; see "Criticism in a Mass Society," in *The Intent of the Critic,* ed. Donald A. Stauffer (Princeton: Princeton University Press), p. 137.

the Catholic doctrine that original sin represents the withdrawal of a "further gift" bestowed by God upon man, rather than a corruption of his essential nature, this being the Protestant view. It is the Protestant view that Auden accepts. "The Sea and the Mirror" suggests that "the human effort to make its own fortune" must always lead us astray and into idolatry: the consequence of our fallen state when unredeemed by faith is that we mistake for the Logos the voices of our own despair.

Where, then, does the Logos come from? The poem does not so much answer this question as direct our attention to where the answer lies, to the real world outside itself, where, now disenchanted and aware of the threatening abyss, we are in a position to hear for the first time the "real Word which is our only *raison d'etre*" and to grasp the significance of that "Wholly Other Life" represented by art. As it began, the section ends conscious of itself and of its audience's relation to its figurative order, and by this device solves, perhaps, the dilemma of the artist who would represent our "condition of estrangement from the truth." Auden's conception of art, particularly as applied to *The Tempest,* resembles Sir Philip Sidney's assertion that art sets before man "another nature" which is the image of his perfection. But for Auden such an image is an imperative, and in this connection the artist confronts a dilemma. The more clearly he indicates the truth, the more removed his picture becomes from the actual conditions of existence, while "the more truthfully he paints the condition, the less clearly can he indicate the truth from which it is estranged":

> . . . worse still, the more sharply he defines the estrangement itself—and, ultimately, what other aim and justification has he, what else exactly *is* the artistic gift which he is forbidden to hide, if not to make you unforgettably conscious of the ungarnished offended gap between what you so questionably are and what you are commanded without any question to become, of the unqualified No that opposes your step in any direction?—the more he must strengthen your delusion that an awareness of

> the gap is in itself a bridge, your interest in your imprisonment a release . . .

The artist can only hope, Auden suggests, "that some unforeseen mishap will intervene to ruin his effect, without, however, obliterating . . . the expectation aroused by him that there was an effect to ruin." And this, as Auden interprets *The Tempest,* is the final significance of Caliban. The one unassimilable element in a world where time and space are infinitely manageable, so that all is subordinate to "the general will to compose, to form at all costs a felicitous pattern," he is the bit of sea condensed on the mirror, the "unpredictable misting over" of Shakespeare's glass, which ruins his effect, though without obliterating the expectation aroused by him that there was an effect to ruin. It is also the significance of Auden's Caliban, whose speech, refusing us the privilege to contemplate our estrangement aesthetically, forestalls the illusion that we have crossed a bridge, and leaves us staring at the offended gap.

Auden's Christianity results, it should be clear, in little divergence from former habits of analysis. Divided consciousness remains the primary fact of the human situation and, as a conception, the principal means of examining experience; the only major difference is that the object of his faith is no longer Natural Law, but Divine Will, a distinction crystallized in the suggestion, from "In Sickness and in Health," that we find salvation "Not by our choice but our consent." Achieved within an existential framework of inquiry, this conception of the Necessary is supported, at the start, with a minimum insistence upon orthodoxy. The problem of identifying the Necessary is the major stumbling block in existential thought, and Auden's first response was to accept the problem as a condition of the existential predicament. Certainly, lying behind "The Quest" is what he summarizes, in 1941, as the moral of Kafka: " 'To be saved is to have Faith, and to have Faith means to recognize something as the Necessary. Whether or not the faith of an individual is misplaced does not matter; indeed, in an absolute sense, it always is . . .' " By 1944, however, he is developing a more stringent viewpoint. He argues that though existentialism begins with "man's immediate experience as a *subject*," it does not abandon the search for a sharable truth, that "it is precisely in the interest of such a common truth, that it is necessary for the individual to begin by learning to be objective about his subjectivity." By 1950, he has decided that the need for engagement must yield to the need for truth:

> A purely existentialist attitude, since it has no conception of the universal or the eternal, cannot be Christian, to whom the existential is only one, admittedly very important aspect of his situation. Atheist existentialism, while more logical, suffers under the disadvantage that, like Stoicism, it can only be held either by madmen, to whom the choice of engagement is arbitrary, or by the fortunate—those whose engagement has been chosen for them by their natural gifts and the chance of history.[19]

Because Auden's faith rests, ultimately, on the authority of Christian revelation, it is appropriate that "For the Time Being," although the title poem, should have come after "The Sea and the Mirror," as if in explanation and elaboration, in the original publication of 1944. The two poems are artistically independent, but the saga of Caliban and Ariel is a work of religious rather than of specifically Christian faith. Auden's Christman oratorio, identifying the Absurd claiming our faith as the Incarnation, fulfills the need to tell us more about the "real Word which is our only *raison d'etre*." This poem is his affirmation that the Word not only is, but is what an Orthodox Christianity conceives it to be: as Simeon reflects, ". . . of this Child it is the case that He is in no sense a symbol." Nevertheless, perhaps in response to the convert's need to

[19] Auden's comments may be found, respectively, in "The Wandering Jew," *New Republic,* CIV (Feb. 1941), p. 185; "A Preface to Kierkegaard," p. 683; and "Religion and the Intellectuals," *Partisan Review,* XVII (Feb. 1950), p. 124.

articulate and confirm his commitment intellectually, the poem does not hesitate to interpret the Incarnation symbolically, as signifying the reconciliation of self and ego, matter and mind, science and art. Auden contends that secular outlooks are unable to cope with the "anxiety in time" which is the chief problem of human existence. Faith is the answer to our "catastrophic situation": as the Word made Flesh, the Incarnation furnishes a pattern for and attests to the meaningfulness of our lives in time.

As Richard Hoggart observes, Auden conceives the historical setting of the Incarnation in terms directly applicable to our own time. He has said that the event occurred "precisely at that moment in history when an impasse seemed to have been reached,"[20] and in the first sestina of "Kairos and Logos," this is treated in terms of the conflict between pagan Rome and ascetic Judaism. "For the Time Being," however, is only nominally set in Palestine. Few poets are as gifted as Auden in discriminating the historical import of the topical, and he is equally adept, chiefly by means of strategies of anachronism, at translating the past into terms of present relevance. Like his treatment of *The Tempest,* his handling of the nativity story is parabolic. It is suggested that the birth of the Child is the experience confronting us each Christmas, and references to Roman rule are to be regarded as vehicles of a metaphor whose tenor is in the present.

In personifying the modern state as Caesar, Auden's satire rests on the important distinction between nature and history. *Nature* is Caliban's realm, where things happen because they have to, and in their malign aspect must be endured as tribulations. Here "time turns round itself in an obedient circle": we eat and sleep, rest and labor, are born and die—"the pattern composed/ By the ten thousand odd things that can possibly happen/ Is permanent in a general average way." On the other hand, *history* is shaped by our choices; it is the realm of unique events that we enter when

[20] "The Means of Grace," p. 765.

nature—our own as well as external nature—has become subject to will, and fate is "no longer a fiat of Matter but a freedom of Mind," tribulations having become temptations. The danger under Caesar is that, in the absence of ultimate goals, the temptation to mere efficiency will become too great and the freedom of the individual be swallowed by the State. Caesar's "Kingdoms" are the areas of nature already organized in this way, and the contrast is pointed between his "Summons" and the message of the star. In the interests of order, personal choice may vanish completely and an authoritarian State do our living for us.

The opening, however, evidences the failure of secular society to give meaning to existence. "Darkness and snow descend/ On all personality"—throughout the section, the prevailing impression is of a discipline having reached the limits of its capacity and now in danger of collapse. Unable to give Eros fulfillment, secular society sustains itself by keeping Eros at bay:

> Outside the civil garden
> Of every day of love there
> Crouches a wild passion
>   To destroy and be destroyed.
> O who to boast their power
> Have challenged it to charge?

The situation presented is one of collective despair, to which the alternative posed is faith. Despair is the experience of being awakened to the Void, to a universe suddenly grown transparent to the accustomed content of the familiar and no longer corroborating the reality of the self; it is a response to our freedom of choice and can be overcome only by evidence that what we do ultimately matters, that temporal life stands in relation to the eternal. Although the Incarnation is this evidence, Auden's modern Romans demand certainty, a miracle to force belief, whereas faith can come only by a leap, when they are fully aware of their despair. Defining our place in the Chain of Being, the chorus points out that it is our desire for truth that drives us into illusion, that the lower orders are closer to possessing what they are unaware they lack. Longing to relate himself to the eternal, man falls into error by his very capacity for longing.

"The Annunciation" introduces his divided faculties. They are Intuition, Feeling, Sensation, and Thought, united before the Fall but now at variance, although his only means of contact with truth, upon the basis of whose evidence he as a volitional creature must act. Appropriately, the vision of Thought is one of pure form divorced from the actuality of becoming, so that Zeno's paradox is uncontested and nothing can be "stated or constructed"; but the "wanton dreams" of the others elude interpretation. Sensation's passage calls to mind the work of John the Baptist, and scattered references to the union of disparate natures suggest a distorted recognition of the Incarnation. But the only thing unmistakable is the impression of disorder, of faculties out of touch with each other and misleading. By contrast, the garden, where Mary wanders in the "sleep of childhood," is symbolic of unified being, which Mary retains as she wakens from sleep into faith,[21] to heal by a consent of will the breech created by the Fall. Auden represents Adam's sin as, in Niebuhrian terms, "pride"—the attempt to deny his creatureliness and "choose his own necessity." Eve's sin is "sensuality"—the effort to retreat from freedom into creaturely self-love. Rejoicing to accept the Word, Mary shows that the contradiction between freedom and finitude is solved by faith. For all classes and temperaments, the union of Word and Flesh sanctions the possibility of a balanced existence.

In the "At the Manger" section, a wedding of Word and Flesh on the level of ordinary humanity is symbolically effected, but in "The Summons" and "The Vision of the Shepherds" we meet the partners to this marriage in unhappy isolation. In the language of "The Sea and the Mirror," the Wise Men are those who have given

[21] Cf. Kierkegaard's statement that "faith is not the first immediacy but a subsequent immediacy." (*Fear and Trembling,* p. 92.)

their all to Ariel: the first, having spent his time seeking Truth in the scientific study of nature, has forgotten the importance of truth in his own life; the second has so devoted himself to barren speculation about progress as to fail to live in the present; the third has neglected to be loving himself because wholly given over to considering the principles of benevolence. All have detached themselves from life in order to observe it and follow the nativity star "To discover how to be human now." The message they are given is "Descend into the fosse of Tribulation," and the echo of Conrad is pertinent: they must submit their dreams to the vicissitudes of existence.

The three Shepherds are representatives of the nonintellectual Caliban element in man. They are those who labor with their hands, performing the menial tasks which, although often unnoticed, keep civilization running. In a somewhat surprising throwback to the categories of Auden's Marxist thinking, they are presented as members of an underprivileged working class who, in possession of the Word, may hope to flourish not as the masses, but as themselves. When Shepherds and Wise Men symbolically meet, the latter, having travelled for many days, have reached finally a symbolic point of rest; the former, after living the same day over and over again, have been granted widened horizons; one group renounces the longing to escape necessity, the other the habit of ignoring the possible. The message of Love is that mind and body mutually co-inhere, that in each of us individually the Word may be made Flesh.

Quite properly, the poem's symbolic action comes to a climax at the manger, in the presence of the Child whose nativity is ritually celebrated. The doctrinal implications of this event Auden explores in "The Meditation of Simeon," concerned with the qualifications of the particular moment in history when the Incarnation occurred. This is a complex section, composed of thirteen separate passages methodically organized in terms of the three Kierkegaardian stages, and it not only formulates what is for Auden the central relevance of Christianity, but places his religious outlook into relation with former orientations. Groupings in this section are indicated by the parallel construction of related passages; perhaps the following chart will be helpful to show the arrangement:

1.–3. } The Aesthetic Approach

4.–6. } The Ethical Approach

7. Summary: THE ABSURDITY OF THE INCARNATION

8. As Revealing the Way of Religious Truth

9.–10. } As replacing the views of (a) Aesthetics (b) Ethics

11.–12. } As compared in import to (a) Aesthetics (b) Ethics

13. As Affirmed in Faith

The substance of Simeon's reflection is that the Incarnation could not take place until it seemed both necessary and impossible, the only antidote to despair and yet a prospect wholly absurd—to be accepted in defiance of reason on the basis of faith. The first criterion could not be met until the effects of the Fall had been clearly realized, a process delayed by the inherent limitations of the Aesthetic way of life. In Kierkegaard's view, the Aesthetic is the category of sensual experience and its immediate derivatives, with its values indicated by the formulas "pleasure/pain," "interesting/uninteresting." Aesthetic talents are inborn gifts rather than acquired skills; the only thing Aesthetics is interested in acquiring is fresh experience or a greater degree of self-expression; it lacks the conception of the self being committed to anything beyond the self *as given* on which to predicate existence. Aesthetics, for this reason, is primarily the category of immediacy: like unfallen man who unthinkingly fulfilled an "order in which desire . . . rejoiced to be reflected," the Aesthetic individual endeavors to live within the confines of the passing moment. And, according to Kierkegaard, "*the view of life natural to immediacy* is one based on fortune." Since the Aesthetic individual fails to reflect upon his condition, he views events as the product of fate and is peculiarly unfit to deal with suffering: "Misfortune is like a narrow pass on the way; now the immediate individual is in it, but his view of life must essentially always tell him that the difficulty will soon cease to hinder, because it is a foreign element."[22]

To Aesthetic man, then, the advent of self-consciousness and the fall into sin could only be regarded as a temporary condition. So long as he remained biologically tied to nature, or unpracticed in the refinements of sensation, or still restricted in the exercise of his gifts, he was bound to hope that his discomfort would either pass of itself (that the Fall had not occurred in fact), or open the way to more mature delights (that the Fall had occurred by necessity), or vanish at the application of the proper formula (that the Fall had occurred by accident). Like the early Auden heroes who seek salvation in another country, the Aesthetic individual trusts that anxiety is avoidable, that suffering is an intrusion upon normalcy. The Incarnation, renewing the promise of Eternal Being, could not occur until it was first understood that Paradise had been lost.

As Auden points out in his edition of Kierkegaard,[23] the Aesthetic view characterized the period of the Greek gods, with its

[22] *Concluding Unscientific Postscript,* trans. David F. Swenson (Princeton: Princeton University Press, 1944), p. 388. Kierkegaard remarks more succinctly (p. 398): "Aesthetically, suffering stands in an accidental relation to existence."

[23] This volume—*The Living Thoughts of Kierkegaard* (New York: David McKay, 1952)—is a helpful guide to Auden's use of Kierkegaard, particularly the introduction, where Auden approaches the categories "historically, i.e., by considering the Aesthetic and the Ethical at stages when each was a religion."

deification of the passions and reverence for the strong. With a greater development of self-consciousness, it gave way to the Ethical outlook of Greek philosophy and the conviction that, however necessary, the redemption of the finite world was impossible. Released to move through time free from the tyranny of the senses, mind could now envision perfection only as an attribute of eternal forms. Confronting the problem of the One and the Many, reason could either affirm the reality of changeless being and deny the evidence of sensation, or admit that all was flux and its own intuition of unity an illusion: that the Infinite could in some way combine with the Finite was unimaginable. As indicated before, this conception of the Ethical as the category of abstract intellect is rather different from that of Kierkegaard, for whom the Ethical is the category of duty. But Auden's view, as well as indicating his opposition to dualism, makes a Kierkegaardian point[24]—that Greek ethical philosophy lacked an adequate understanding of the will and, therefore, of sin, which only Christian revelation could supply. Thus, before this revelation could take place, it was necessary that Ethical man extend as far as secularly possible his knowledge of good and evil, so that the only thing remaining unknown to him would be his "Original Sin," which is "itself what conditions his will to knowledge." He could then maintain, as did Socrates, that sin was simply ignorance. The first act of sin having occurred through the agency of an unconscious self-deception, he could not see that sin might be to know the good and yet require divine aid to will it.

It should be observed at this point that Auden's Christian view of things, with this insistence on the fallen will, even as it indicates the reason for his retreat from a secular faith in "knowledge," in essence only carries to a conclusion longstanding secular discernments. The observation that thinking tends to be "interested"

[24] Cf. "The Socratic Definition of Sin," in *The Sickness Unto Death*, pp. 218-27.

thinking, with its sources in Freud and in Marx, has always been for him, as we have seen, a major insight into the problem of evil, and it is precisely the insight confirmed by the doctrine of Original Sin. The doctrine indicates the fact that sin, in Kierkegaard's words, "presupposes itself," that the sinful will is operative, not only in our conscious choices, but unconsciously, in the prior consciousness of choice by which it justifies itself.[25] Auden's contention that the Tree of the Knowledge of Good and Evil is a devil's fiction—a projection of our anxiety—even as it undermines the adequacy of Freudian and Marxist solutions, acknowledges their common premise as a fact of life. In the absence of Grace, our thinking must always be, in the pejorative sense, "interested" thinking, corrupted by self-love, or, as he puts it from a somewhat different angle, interpreting Kafka: "Man can never know the whole truth, because as the subject who knows, he has to remain outside the truth, and the truth is therefore incomplete." The only guarantee that he is going right is—"that he fails to get anywhere."[26] For this reason, we are told earlier in the poem:

> . . . the garden is the only place there is, but
> you will not find it
> Until you have looked for it everywhere and found
> nowhere that is not a desert;
> The miracle is the only thing that happens, but
> to you it will not be apparent,

[25] In "The Means of Grace" (p. 766), Auden quotes with approval Niebuhr's definition of Original Sin as *"a symbol of an aspect of every historical moment in the life of a man . . . Perfection before the Fall is, in other words, perfection before the act."* Auden has dramatized this concept in the opening poem of the *"Horae Canonicae"* sequence.

[26] "K's Quest," in *The Kafka Problem,* ed. Angel Flores (New York: New Directions, 1946), p. 52. Cf. Kafka, whose "Reflections," among other things, have influenced Auden: "Truth is indivisible, hence it cannot recognize itself; anyone who wants to recognize it has to be a lie." This passage is from *Dearest Father,* trans. Ernst Kaiser and Eithne Wilkins (New York: Schocken Books, 1954), p. 43.

> Until all events have been studied and nothing
> happens that you cannot explain.

We are advised to "see without looking, hear without listening"; we are in the truth only when, in faith, we are conforming to a Truth beyond our comprehension.

Acknowledging that the Incarnation could not take place until it was understood to be both necessary and impossible, Simeon declares his faith in the Absurd. Of the four passages analyzing the Religious outlook, the first two treat the Christian revelation as resolving the dilemma of temporal life. Contrasting the Aesthetic view of existence as controlled by the arbitrary content of the passing moment, so that the "temporal succession of events has no meaning,"[27] Simeon reflects that "By the event of this birth the true significance of all other events is defined." Furthermore, in opposition to Ethics, which regards ignorance as sin rather than as temptation, Religion reveals that we are fated to choose—that insofar as "each man loves God and through Him his neighbor," we are free to conquer nature and transmute time into history. As Auden observes in "Canzone," "Love . . . asks its images for more than love"; the reference is to *agape,* "Eros mutated by Grace," which lifts us beyond the predictable self-love of the creatures. When Auden occasionally points out that poetry is "frivolous" or a "game," it is in consequence of the belief that only our duty to love can ultimately be considered serious.

Yet Christianity appeals to him by the quality of its worldliness —he notes that though the Church has often been dualistic, it is only since Christendom that dualism has been seen as something to attack.[28] As Simeon represents it, the significance of the Word made Flesh is that in their mergence the claims of both matter and spirit are vindicated. No longer is it possible (Aesthetically) to judge individuals according to the marks of fortune or situations

[27] *Living Thoughts,* introduction, p. 10.
[28] "The Means of Grace," p. 765.

by their outward interest; we are all potentially tragic as we inwardly confront temptation in our fallen state and all, as well, bungling fairy tale protagonists accomplishing our tasks only with the aid of Grace. Nor may we any longer (Ethically) regard finite nature as illusory, and truth as the exclusive possession of philosophers, or think that God as an immutable Idea transcends the world, indifferent to its needs. Showing that Word and Flesh are mutually fulfilling, that our passions have purpose and knowledge a real object, Christian revelation sanctions the development of both Science and Art.

A comic triumph and itself a meditation of sorts, the speech of Herod, standing in opposition to Simeon's, gives another view of the Incarnation, this one, Auden realizes, most likely our own. It has for a model the *Meditations* of Marcus Aurelius, which also begin by giving thanks to benefactors:

> From Appolonius I learned freedom of will and undeviating steadiness of purpose; and to look to nothing else, not even for a moment, except to reason . . .[29]

The parallel has its point, for Herod is a "liberal," who wants everyone to be happy and who takes his stand towards this end in the efficacy of reason and the benefits of mass education. In the end, Auden succeeds in rendering Herod's situation and, hence, his position ridiculous, but he is satirizing attitudes recently his own and it is not entirely a straw man who falls. If under Herod children exist "who have never seen a louse, shopkeepers who have never handled a counterfeit coin, women of forty who have never hidden in a ditch except for fun," this is undeniably to the good. Nor is Herod unaware of how little he has actually accomplished, how much remains to be done if the "Rational Life" is to be made accessible to all. If he equates the coming of Christ with such

[29] *The Stoic and Epicurean Philosophers,* ed. Whitney J. Oates (New York: The Modern Library, 1957), p. 492.

things as ouija-boards and fairies, this reenforces an import of the Joseph section:

> *Joseph, you have heard*
> *What Mary says occurred;*
> *Yes, it may be so.*
> *Is it likely? No.*

Auden means to acknowledge that, from the standpoint of both reason and common sense, the idea of an incarnate God is indeed absurd. He has defined humanism as "government of the ego by the ego for the ego."[30] Herod's problem is that he is up against a truth greater than he can understand.

The "Flight into Egypt," however, depicts the uneasy triumph of Herod's point of view, the exile of Christ effected by our secularization and felt as a state of alienation from God. Auden has remarked that the desert is a place of temptation, and that "only the individual or community with the faith and courage which can dare, endure, and survive its trials is worthy to enter into the promised land of the New Life."[31] The voices of the desert belong to those who have fallen by the wayside, who have accepted as a refuge rather than as a trial the desert's "unending wastes of delirium." But the desert may be overcome:

> Skulls recurring every mile
> Direct the thirsty to the Nile;
>
> And the jackal's eye at night
> Forces Error to keep right.

The contention, once again, is that faith is found only in the "Kingdom of Anxiety"—which is to say, only when one has fully experienced the aloneness and the barrenness of a life from which faith is absent.

[30] Foreword to Emile Cammaerts, *The Flower of Grass* (New York: Harper & Brothers, 1945), p. xiii.

[31] *The Enchafèd Flood,* pp. 24-25.

Auden points out that life, unlike art, is not a game; we cannot say, "I will live on condition that I have a talent for living." Those with authentic talent are perhaps the saints: released from anxiety by the power of faith, they are free to live in the present and to accept the world in the spirit of *agape;* for it cannot be stressed too often that Auden's Christianity offers little encouragement to asceticism:

> Our bodies cannot love:
> But, without one,
> What works of Love could we do?[32]

For the rest of us, so long as we live we are in the grips of existential obligation. The Necessary imposed by the mere fact of our being, of our being particular individuals, is that we consent to be ourselves, exist as particular selves rather than as members of a "Public" or victims of despair. "How shall we live?" has always been, of course, the question for Auden, but the movement towards Christianity entailed a greater responsiveness to the uniqueness of individuals and the complications of living, and the result of having found answers for himself is that he is less doctrinaire. After the allegorical excursions of "The Sea and the Mirror" and "For the Time Being," he seems to have felt it necessary to turn to a more directly representational level of portrayal, to confront the dilemmas of ordinary individuals with particular endowments, as they face the actual world. The result was *The Age of Anxiety* (1947).[33]

The poem opens in a New York bar where four characters have gathered for refuge against the pressures of war time. Successful

32 "Postscript" to "The Cave of Nakedness," *About the House* (New York: Random House, 1965), p. 34. For the contrast between life and gamesmanship, see "Postcript: The Frivolous & the Earnest," *The Dyer's Hand,* p. 431.

33 This is the date of the American edition (New York: Random House); quotations in this chapter are from the British edition (London: Faber and Faber, 1948).

and intelligent, Malin is a medical officer in the Canadian Air Force; Emble is a young American in the Navy; Quant, a widower and eldest of the lot, is a shipping-office clerk, by common standards of success a failure; Rosetta is an emigre from England prospering as buyer for a department store. Each is discontented and lonely and when the radio interrupts their private reveries, they fall to talking and agree to discuss their human predicament ("The Seven Ages"); afterwards, they share in a semi-intoxicated dream-vision quest for happiness ("The Seven Stages") and finally adjourn to Rosetta's apartment for sandwiches and a nightcap before parting.

The poem is concerned with the individual's need to accept and be himself if his life is to have meaning, and the "Prologue" finds each character absorbed in meditation revealing his refusal or inability to do so. In Quant's case, there is "no one-to-one correspondence between his social or economic position and his private mental life," and we find him engaged in self-questioning, staring into the mirror whimsically addressing his image, as if it enjoyed what Quant himself pretends he does not need, "Some shadowy she who shares in my absence,/ Enjoys my jokes." Quant himself is "The marked man of romantic thrillers," for whom woman's love would be dangerous—or so he says, deriving some ironic satisfaction from the awareness that he is trying to shrug off his unhappiness by playing a game which dramatizes it.

Malin is the intellectual of the group and the closest to a real awareness of the human predicament. In many respects, he voices Auden's own views, his thoughts centering on man rather than on his own person. His fragmentary musings on the Chain of Being as reformulated by modern science are characteristic; atom, plant and beast all are bound on different levels by a law of being; only man "has no mean" and must choose his fate; hence his anxiety, a distinctively human affliction which Rosetta attempts to escape by conjuring up day-dreams of a placid English countryside where "work and law and guilt are just literary words," as in a detective story before the discovery of the body. It is the same affliction which Emble projects onto the future. Good looking and sexually successful, he is youthfully insecure about his real abilities and, as a result, overly disdainful of the commonplace. As Emble watches the other occupants of the bar, the failures and the malcontents "who might have been/ The creative odd ones the average need/ To suggest new goals," his bitterness, though he is not fully aware of this, reflects the fear that he is observing his own fate.

The characters' thoughts soon turn to the war. Although Auden's descriptions have been criticized, Rosetta's passage finely exemplifies the complicated state vividly evoked by a flash of telling detail:

> Arrogant officers, armed in cars,
> Go roaring down roads on the wrong side.

As for the many periphrases, these, when coupled with the effect of the alliterative line, do much to render the impersonality of modern warfare and the musing detachment afforded by time:

> Strained with gazing
> Our eyes ached, and our ears as we slept
> Kept their care for the crash that would turn
> Our fears into fact. In the fourth watch
> A torpedo struck on the port bow:
> The blast killed many; the burning oil
> Suffocated some; some in lifebelts
> Floated upright till they froze to death;
> The younger swam but the yielding waves
> Denied help; they were not supported,
> They swallowed and sank, ceased thereafter
> To appear in public; exposed to snap
> Verdicts of sharks, to vague inquiries
> Of ameoboid monsters, mobbed by slight
> Unfriendly fry, refused persistence.
> They are nothing now but names assigned to
> Anguish in others, areas of grief.
> Many have perished; more will.

The alliterative line, with its heavy stresses falling often on words of small content, subverts the process by which facts become ordered into the expression of feelings. But, as in early Auden, the result is an emphasis on the thingness of things—here the bluntness and finality of events ("They swallowed and sank"). The contribution of periphrasis is to establish an angle of inquiry supplying ironic perspective; greeted by the wrong public, the sailor-celebrities seem victims of a characteristic human capriciousness. As background to the poem, the war furnishes a sense of the apartness of our lives from any principle of meaning.

When the radio interrupts, the characters are impelled to speak their thoughts. "A crime has occurred, accusing all," says Malin, recalling "New Year Letter" and revealing the degree to which he is Auden's spokesman. And the four proceed to exchange their views, which for the most part Auden would uphold, although each is also character-revealing. To Emble, who is young, the war is the protection of a better culture against "barbarian misrule," an effort vindicated by the fate of defenseless civilizations from the antique past. Malin's comment is that the barbarian of the present is no invader from the wilderness but a homegrown, factory-bred product. With little to look back or ahead to, Quant sees things cynically; the war is simply a "defence of friends against foes' hate," and he believes that the aftermath will be dismal; values will have perished and behavior will reflect this; in the wake of the conqueror's triumphal car will come the "Public hangman, the private wastrel." Rosetta's view is equally gloomy, for despite her escapist daydreams, her temperament is essentially realistic: there will be "more deaths/ and worse wars," she believes; the peace will be plagued by the unlaid ghosts of the past.

The radio this time brings a noisy commercial, and suggesting they continue their talk in a booth, Malin proposes as subject their own plight, the "incessant Now of/ The traveller through time," his quest for the "Absconded self" he must will to become. In a few lines Malin summarizes Auden's Christian conception of man, who must live his life partly in nature and time, as self, and partly transcending it, as ego. As a result, he is "at once/ Outside and inside his own demand/ For personal pattern," and though able to "explain every/ What in this world," unable to find a place for himself or to understand his original sin, the "insoluble/ Final fact" of guilt resulting, as Niebuhr had shown, from the inevitable failure of his fallen will to attain the perfection which as transcendent ego he thinks possible for himself. And so his anxiety.

> At not being what he knows that before
> This world was he was willed to become.

The solution as Auden sees it is, of course, faith; only with faith is it possible to accept the self as it is and, consenting to the will of God, choose the self that, "by omission and stress," one is required to become. But it is a solution his characters will be unable to reach.

So "The Seven Ages" trace the course of life, not as it should be, but as it is for the anxious many who have failed to come to proper terms with it. Malin provides a theoretical understanding, while the comments of the others, being personal, reveal the nature of their failings. The first age described is childhood though, strictly speaking, it is preceded by a period of innocence when, a "pantheist not a solipsist," and unable to distinguish between himself and his environment, the infant is "Righteous still." It is only with the sense of self allowing the first deliberate act that:

> He jumps and is judged; he joins mankind,
> The fallen families, freedom lost,
> Love become Law.

From this point on, the "Way" will always appear something exacted in the face of temptation rather than the spontaneous choice of innate desire.

In the period of childhood proper, the individual "looks at grown-ups/ With conscious care," but, despite this, existence is mainly immediate, tied to the "Instant present." Because of the strong influence of imagination on the shadowy inner life of "Feelings through facts," this is the period of solipsism, for Quant a time when tires could be "burned alive," for Emble when he could bring punishment from heaven upon tormenting cousins, for Rosetta when her "dearest doll was deaf and spoke in/ Grunts like grandfather." Convincingly typical as they are, there is a glimpse of the older person in each of these reminiscences. In Quant's case, it is simply that the grimy unpromising environment of childhood foreshadows the beaten man, but Emble's delusion of exceptional powers and Rosetta's belief in secret arrangements already indicate the devices they will use to keep from self-acceptance.

The second age is adolescence—that coming not of consciousness but of *self*-consciousness—which punctures the childhood dream and reveals the presence of Caliban:

> Thus woken, he is
> Amused no more by the merely given
> Felt fact, the facile emergence of
> Thought with thing, but, threatened from all sides,
> Embarrassed by his body's bald statements,
> His sacred soul obscenely tickled
> And bellowed at by a blatant Without . . .

This is the normal beginning of "The Journey of life," and appropriately Malin's comments shift from the imagery of "jump" to that of "pilgrimage"; but to envision the journey is not necessarily to set out. Auden presents adolescence as a time of self-pity and of the fantasies it breeds. It was the period when Quant as a sullen busboy imagined himself a rich tycoon with sirens at his disposal, when Emble, after an argument with his father, again consoled himself with melodramatic visions of grandeur. For Rosetta, characteristically, the fantasy was of a big house offering station and security.

Love makes its appearance in the next age of young manhood or womanhood and, although experienced as an obstacle on the path, brings a step closer the world of reality soon to be faced. Malin's comments are obscure here and, like all the songs in the poem, those of Rosetta and Emble strain for effects which in the end are not revealing; but the shared experience is clearly disillusionment in love. Because the images which haunt are now of real others, sooner or later the deceptions practiced by imagination are exposed and, "learning to love," the individual is taught "To know he does not." The proper reaction is Sebastian's, to "Shake Failure's bruising fist!" For the disbelieving Quant, this has been the process of equating love with lust.

The fourth age leaves behind "the humourless places/ His dreams would prefer" and marks the beginning of adult responsibility:

> By the water's edge
> The unthinking flood . . .
> . . . .
> The real world of
> Theology and horses . . .

Now we are required to come to terms with things as they are, for in the fifth age of full maturity we will live in the world we have come to recognize, and the spirit in which we accept things will decide our fate. For Rosetta and Emble, the issue is still open, though at this point her response is defiance: "Too soon we embrace that/ Impermanent appetitive flux"—or, more bluntly (replying to Quant):

> I refuse to accept
> Your plain place, your unprivileged time.
> . . . .
> As life after life lapsing out of
> Its essential self sinks into
> One press-applauded public untruth . . .

But instead of choosing to be herself in spite of pressures to join the "Public," Rosetta attempts to escape from herself in regressive fantasies. Emble's response is similar, for he too fears that to accept the age is to be enslaved by it, to stagnate in a mediocrity so enervating that only the thought of "some great suffering" brings relief. So he views the future with dread: "Will nightfall bring us/ Some awful order—Keep a hardware store/ In a small town . . . Teach science for life to/ Progressive girls—?" Though inwardly aware that he has little in common with the "princes of fiction," Emble deals with his youthful lack of assurance by pretending that he is the exceptional individual, awaiting a knowledge of his mission. Kierkegaard provides a relevant irony: "Those . . . who carry the jewel of faith are likely to be delusive, because their outward appearance bears an eternal resemblance to . . . Philistinism."[34]

Of the older two, Malin belongs to the fortunate minority who, having accepted their world, have made a success of it. He is one of those discussed in the "Prologue" who in times of peace "wake up each morning excited by the prospect of another day of interesting and difficult work," and for whom the day of reckoning is postponed, unless peace should give way to war and an anxiety forcing self-questioning. Quant is a confessed failure for whom the notion of self as a distinct and personal identity is without validity. "We are mocked by unmeaning," he believes, and his error is that he has accepted the world as imaged by his own despair. In a moving passage of acute insight on Auden's part, Quant predicts for Emble a similar defeatist submission, when

> The train-ride between your two natures,
> The morning-evening moment when
> You are free to reflect on your faults still,
> Is an awkward hiatus, is indeed
> The real risk to be read away with
> Print and pictures . . .

With forced indifference, Quant declares his belief in the futility

[34] *Fear and Trembling*, p. 49.

of existence. We live in nature, without free will, and history is impossible: "We move on/ As the wheel wills; one revolution/ Registers all things . . ."

With the next period begins the decline of old age, accompanied (inevitably in light of the past) by dissatisfaction and discontent. Childhood hurts seem still unhealed, a meaningful existence now out of reach. The individual regrets his life and pines, says Malin, "for some/ Nameless Eden where he never was." Despite his cynicism, Quant admits that he has known such a wish and, recounting his quest for the fairy-tale treasure, he concedes in a rare moment his consciousness of guilt. Rosetta and Emble join in the lament, he for the "garden," she for the magical innocence of a play-thing world, experiences enjoyed only recently, or so they think, still feeling the impact of adolescent disillusion. Malin goes on to the Seventh Age, one of decrepitude with "little to say," and the discussion ends.

As Monroe Spears points out,[35] having concluded their survey and done much to illuminate their failings, all the characters ironically hasten back to their individual illusions. Rosetta again thinks of the eccentrically happy lives of the leisured, Quant reverts into protective cynicism, and Emble to his Prospero's fear of being "a mere one among many." In this unpromising condition they undertake the dream exploration they hope will lead to the "Quiet Kingdom" where happiness is.

Richard Hoggart expresses what many must feel when he observes that, though we may be clear as to the "general import of the 'Seven Stages,' the significance of each is unjustifiably hard to discover."[36] Particularly at the beginning, the speeches have the character of stage directions, but the settings they establish, symbolic in intention, lack the "mana" of symbol and elicit behavior

[35] "The Dominant Symbols in Auden's Poetry," *Sewanee Review,* LIX (Summer 1951), p. 421.

[36] *Auden: An Introductory Essay* (London: Chatto & Windus, 1951), p. 202.

seeming neither inevitable, nor even particularly appropriate. There undoubtedly exists a key to these mysteries which someone will discover. The present difficulty is that interpretation seems so necessary if the existence of the section is to be justified, and that meaning comes at present, and very imperfectly, only from the willed efforts of the reader as, in detachment, he attempts to juggle details into an intelligible pattern. The section does not fare well under T. S. Eliot's observation that great poetry communicates before it is fully understood.

Although the explanation leaves much unsolved, it may be suggested that the "Stages" depict, not stages of spiritual progress or stages of a lifetime, so much as modes of being or, perhaps better, of knowing, that we experience and rely on moving from sleep through the course of a normal day, each representing a different level of human resource to be soberly examined and found inadequate as a guide to existence. The characters are in search of the Earthly Paradise, which they will not find; because they lack the courage to leap, the only human resource they will fail to test is faith.

The first stage represents the racial unconscious and reaches back into pre-history. We begin with a salt lake, the origins of life, and move gradually onward amidst increasing signs of habitation and ascending levels of civilization (nomadic, warrior, agricultural), until the Middle Ages are reached and the long climb towards the conscious condition and our own age begins. That the characters do not find what they seek indicates, perhaps, that they seek a happiness pre-historic in the sense of pre-human; at any rate their condition here antedates the acquisition of personality. The comic petulance displayed is to be justified probably by the antic strategies of the dream convention, but this is one of many occasions when it is difficult to decide precisely how Auden means to be taken. Efforts at explanation in the following may be baldly stated; they are offered in humility.

Having completed their journey in time, the characters notice that "everything seems somehow familiar": "miles inland," or inside the mind, the Mariner's Tavern is the personal unconscious. Here, inhibitions are discarded ("Heroes confess to whores, detectives/ Chat or play chess with thieves") and ideas brew (one hears "the creak of new creeds on the kitchen stairs"). To stay here would be, presumably, to remain in a restless dream condition, and the four quickly set out for the ports, which are the senses and, particularly, the eyes.

Prior to confronting the "out there," each character feels a sense of the dissatisfactions shaping his ordinary experience. Emble complains of the isolating role of "pilgrim prince/ Whose life belongs to his quest," Quant is aware of his guilt, Rosetta threatened by vulgar incursions upon "a land of ease." Malin hopes to find in a glimpse of the ocean (material creation) a clue to man's anxious existence in time. But objective sensory experience cannot be prolonged—at the ports, "they may not linger long"—and the four again turn inland, this time towards the city, which structures reality by offering the habitual roles and pre-formulated values which reduce living to routine and stock response. Even before they arrive, Rosetta announces her contempt, her longing for "anarchic joy," freedom from "public prison," and of course we have heard all this before and it is a measure of the section's failure; for the "Seven Ages," despite the seeming distinction, are actually *stages:* one does not conclude terms with the world with the coming of adulthood; such action *is* the coming of adulthood —and it is not at all clear what the "Stages" set out to accomplish that the earlier section had not already accomplished more comprehensibly and, at times, movingly. It is possibly because Auden was aware of the need to avoid repetition that the "Stages," in spite of length, seem so thin in content.

The fourth stage follows the "tortuous route" of personal memory to a large country house outside the city. Auden's spying out of naughtiness seems somewhat old-maidish here, but Rosetta's disillusionment makes the point that memory too is a deceiver and inadequate guide. The race to the graveyard represents a returning to the accumulated wisdom of the past with the same results; the sixth stage brings the characters to the hermetic gardens.

As Hoggart has observed, "In the gardens, there occurs the moment of illumination and Love, the indication of what may be striven toward."[37] In passage, all four had experienced a sense incompleteness: the garden is the answering state of fulfilling vision, of imagination as it discerns the salvation of the possible. The vision requires action, though, a commitment of will and a leap of faith, and to the four it seems an accusation to be rationalized away. They retire in disorder and soon find they have only the last half of the seventh stage to complete.

This is the desert and, like the one in "For the Time Being," a state of despair which tests as it impels the longing for ultimate meaning. It is the human state exhausted of resources save for the prospect of a leap into faith, but no other's efforts prove that the feat is really possible and, as Emble[38] points out, the barrenness of the waste is such that few can endure the temptation to grasp at any orientation bringing order to existence (here "plates of roasted rats/ Can make the mouth water"). While the characters pause in perplexity, their fate is decided for them. The bar is closing; voices break in upon their dream, "declaring their weak/ Faith in confusion."

In the "Masque," now thrown back upon themselves, the characters attempt to compensate for their disappointment. The casual attraction between Rosetta and Emble becomes the focal point of an alcoholic euphoria in which all share. The section is undoubtedly too long, but fevered animation deftly gives way to a quiet undercutting of exorbitant hopes; returning from seeing the older two of the group down in the elevator, Rosetta finds her prince soundly sleeping. Gently ironic, her self-assessment is the

[37] *Ibid.*, p. 207.

[38] Or possibly Malin—both the Faber and Faber and Random House editions surely err in giving two successive speeches to Emble.

climax of the poem and one of the few examples of human emotion convincingly dramatized. She realizes that however troubled he may be, Emble as a Christian is assured of belonging in a world which for her must always be alien. There could be nothing between them really; try as she may, she cannot keep secrets from God:

> He won't pretend to
> Forget how I began, nor grant belief
> In the mythical scenes I make up
> Of a home like theirs, the Innocent Place where
> His Law can't look . . .

She accepts finally the brick villa and "poky parlour" of her actual childhood and the "poor fat father" to whom she couldn't write. She ends her reflections acknowledging her identity as a Jew: "Hear, O Israel, the Lord our God, the Lord is One."

As Rosetta declares her self-acceptance, Quant and Malin, meditating, bring to an issue the difference between nature and history. His characteristic levity counterpointing his companion's candor, Quant predicts that the present war will conclude as all others, with appropriate gestures and life the same as always: existence is cyclical. Malin agrees that we fail to learn from the past, that our future seems fearful; but his attitude differs. Directed not outside the world but towards the world, Auden's Christian faith is that history is meaningful, moving towards an end which is the coming of God's Kingdom. It is significant that Malin's plea for commitment evokes echoes of the thirties:[39]

> . . . the noble despair of the poets
> Is nothing of the sort; it is silly

---

[39] One thinks of Louis MacNeice's *Autumn Journal:*

> None of our hearts are pure, we always have mixed motives,
> Are self deceivers, but the worst of all
> Deceits is to murmur, "Lord, I am not worthy"
> And, lying easy, turn your face to the wall.

To refuse the tasks of time
And, overlooking our lives,
Cry—"Miserable wicked me,
How interesting I am."
We would rather be ruined than changed,
We would rather die in our dread
Than climb the cross of the moment
And let our illusions die.

Malin admits, however, that he cannot comprehend the paradox of time's relationship with eternity or truly conceive of an order of perfect love. But neither Reason nor Imagination is adequate to this task:

. . . the place of birth
Is too obvious and near to notice,
Some dull dogpatch a stone's throw
Outside the walls, reserved
For the eyes of faith to find.

To be reborn is to experience our "center of volition shifted" ("The Garden"), while Malin has only "negative knowledge," the knowledge that faith is necessary and of how and why, but not the faith itself. It is knowledge that our passions are no more to be relied on than our mental faculties, that they pray not to the Cross or Clarté but to "primitive totems"—although our usual worship is just as deficient, mainly an attempt to deny our creaturely indebtedness to Dame Kind. Once again, then, Auden suggests that Caliban and Ariel must fail us, that only faith can free us from fragmentation. Everything man does, he has written, "from going to the toilet to mathematical speculation, is an act of religious worship, either of God or of himself."[40] Malin asserts that our misery is that we are "Wanting our own way, unwilling to say Yes."

40 "Augustus to Augustine," *New Republic,* CXI (Sept. 1944), p. 374.

Largely because of the flatness of the "Seven Stages," but also because this itself is symptomatic of an essentially static theme, an overall lack of dramatic conflict, it is hard to question the general judgment that *The Age of Anxiety* is not a success. The poem is insufficiently appreciated, for it contains much accomplished verse and a good deal of genuine if somewhat abstract insight into human living; it is difficult to evaluate justly because many of its effects do not simply fail—they alienate. One thinks particularly of what seem the "baroque" elements in Auden's eclogue,[41] the occasions when flippancy is the medium of appraisal and the characters become grotesque, mere masks of themselves. Quant's passages fall regularly into this category, to witness, presumably, a defensive retreat into ironic bravado; but this is also the mode of most of the songs, and it recurs persistently and inopportunely all through the poem, without much reference to the moods of personality.

Spears regards the poem as "mock-heroic," its action a "parody Quest,"[42] and although the terms presumably refer to an irony of situation, the tracing out of an established pattern of action on a level of enactment where proper completion of the pattern is impossible, the fact is that Auden often seems engaged in parody of the more common variety. This is conspicuous in the "Dirge," where the characters express the irksomeness of moral responsibility in a manner recalling the farce techniques of *The Dance of Death* and appropriate to the anonymous chorus of a pageant (Cf. "Great is Caesar"). Such behavior is distinctly unsettling when they are supposed to be ordinary, intelligent, human beings, whose distance from salvation is the desperate predicament char-

[41] As Spears observes, "The trappings of the eclogue are there: the slight dramatic form, with dialogue; the singing contest; an elegy; love-songs and laments, with courtship of a shepherdess; formal 'artificial' diction and meter."—"The Satirist as Lunatic Clergyman," *Sewanee Review,* LIX (Winter 1951), p. 50.

[42] "Dominant Symbols in Auden's Poetry," p. 418.

acterizing our time. An obvious explanation is that Auden fails to respect sufficiently people such as those portrayed. The truth is less disturbing, I suspect. He seems to have committed himself to working with a theme no longer personally compelling, and to have reached that point in coming to terms with his own problems when it was no longer possible to deal with suffering without a sense of the theatrical, if not the melodramatic, and an incongruous need to be funny or ironic.

The choice of a verse form seems unfortunate from this point of view, in that the demands of the alliterative line, drawing the poet's attention to his medium, tend to increase his sense of distance. When the subject is concrete, the danger is minimal, but if a mere feeling of misgiving is to be expressed, Auden seems easily distracted into entertaining himself. And almost any alliterative words will do: "Reproached by the doves/ My groin groans." A facetious idiom intrudes upon even the most successful efforts to render a state of mind:

> You'll build here, be
> Satisfied soon, while I sit waiting
> On my light luggage to leave if called
> For some new exile, with enough clothes
> But no merry maypole.

When single-line interchanges occur, alliteration seems mere silliness:

> Muster no monsters, I'll meeken my own.
>
> You may wish till you waste, I'll want here.
>
> Too blank the blink of these blind heavens.

"What distresses most," says Hoggart, "is that Auden worries his themes, that he seems not to have the patience to let them emerge, but has to thrust them at the reader."[43] The reason, one

[43] *Auden*, p. 211.

suspects, is that nothing is "said" by *The Age of Anxiety* that he had not already said, and at length, in "The Sea and the Mirror" and "For the Time Being." Auden's is a gift relatively indifferent to the intangibilities of character, and this time, one feels, there was little for him to work out and order anew; the delight in symmetry so often before an effective tool of analysis could exercise itself here only in a numerical parallel lacking significance ("Seven Ages," "Seven Stages") and the feeble challenge of exhausting the modes of transportation (airplane, boat, etc.). It should not be surprising that *The Age of Anxiety* prefigures a shift in manner and interest, one entailing a freedom to leave the claims of faith largely unspoken, and to bring humor to bear on our most solemn concerns.

CHAPTER VI

Conclusion: The Poet as Anthropologist

NONES—THE SHIELD OF ACHILLES—HOMAGE TO CLIO—ABOUT THE HOUSE

> . . . I should like
> to be to my water-brethren as a spell
> of fine weather: Many are stupid,
>
> and some, maybe, are heartless, but who is not
> vulnerable, easy to scare,
> and jealous of his privacy?
>
> —"Thanksgiving for a Habitat"

IN *The Age of Anxiety*, Auden was playing, poetically, the role of a former self, that of the convert impelled to ponder the pathways to salvation because not very long ago he himself had been a seeker of the Way. This was a fruitful role in "The Sea and the Mirror" and "For the Time Being." After achieving a basis of faith in Christianity, it was obviously necessary for Auden to validate the grounds of commitment and to formulate belief; the compelling nature of the challenge may be gauged from the intellectual ardor displayed in meeting it—the general provocativeness of these two efforts. By *The Age of Anxiety*, however, the need to vindicate faith seems to have lessened; there is evident in the poem's factitious structure and randomness of tone a restlessness with themes exhausted of their urgency. Having consolidated his gains, Auden was ready for a new role which he had yet to discover.

To characterize fully Auden's new manner and voice is not an easy task. One encounters an intangibility much like the one Kierkegaard confronted when he sat down to record his gratitude to Lessing.[1] He wished to express his appreciation for what Lessing had shown him; namely, the profound inwardness of his God-relationship. But owing to the very nature of this thing, Kierkegaard could not be sure that the quality was actually there in Lessing's work—quite properly, since to the extent that it was demonstrable it could not be inwardness. With regard to what might be called Auden's poetry of "conversion," Kierkegaard would not have been troubled. Particularly with reference to "For the Time Being" and its symbolical exposition of the meaning of the Child who is "in no sense a symbol," Auden's position is closer to that described in another Kierkegaardian parable, again on the subject of religious inwardness, to the position of the man who, having arrived at the truth that a man should have no disciples, begins to preach this truth, and attracts followers (who also begin to preach that a man should have no disciples). Perhaps this is a contradiction implicit in the situation of the convert; but it can no longer be charged to Auden. Today his Christianity controls his outlook even when it is not overtly in view, and, paradoxically, it is more persuasively felt than when Christian themes dominated the surface of his work. His new role is to display a delight in roles—in contrivance, playfulness, and eccentricity—that seems possible only in someone secure in his sense of self, for whom role-playing is no longer a necessity. Though the results are not fully classifiable, Auden today is writing *out of* his Christianity rather than about it.

That his delight in play and a calculated self-exhibitionism has significance in his own eyes may be gathered from Auden's remark that an individual can properly realize himself only if his

[1] See "Something About Lessing," in *Concluding Unscientific Postscript,"* trans. David F. Swenson (Princeton: Princeton University Press, 1944), pp. 59-66.

imagination is at work envisaging those possibilities which for him are "both permissible and real," but that once this faculty has done its work, "to the degree that, with its help, I have become what I should become, imagination has a right to demand its freedom to play without any limitations, for there is no longer any danger that I shall take its play seriously."[2] Riding along "A Permanent Way" (SA), Auden pictures himself able to indulge his fancies whatever they may be, confident that "the good old train will jog/ To the dogma of its rails." There is, today, less sense of the dogmatic in Auden than ever before, but this itself evidences the security of his anchorage in Christianity. His playfulness is the result of an outlook settled in essentials and free to arm itself with whimsy in their defense.

Within this context, we can better understand why he has been increasingly critical of existentialist thinking. Questioning the accuracy of existentialist descriptions of choice, "like Pascal's wager or Kierkegaard's leap," he now admits that he discovered the significance of his own decisive choices only after they were made, that he might never have taken a step had he been fully aware of the risks involved. He has also protested against existentialism's "imaginary anthropology," which tends to exclude from consideration elements such as reason or our physical nature, "about which general statements can be made" (DH, p. 103). From someone whose own work has been founded on existentialist principles, these, no doubt, are surprising observations, but they indicate

2 "Balaam and His Ass," *The Dyer's Hand* (New York: Random House, 1962; London: Faber and Faber, 1963), pp. 133-34 of the American edition. References to the volumes of this period will be given hereafter in the text; the following abbreviations will be used: DH—*The Dyer's Hand;* N—*Nones* (New York: Random House, 1951; London: Faber and Faber, 1952); SA—*The Shield of Achilles* (New York: Random House, 1955; London: Faber and Faber, 1955); HC—*Homage to Clio* (New York: Random House, 1960; London: Faber and Faber, 1960); AH —*About the House* (New York: Random House, 1965; London: Faber and Faber, 1966). With the exception of *Nones,* I have used the American edition in each case.

more than anything else a lessening of the need to justify and apologize. Auden surely knew before making his confession that he had not really taken what seemed at the time a Kierkegaardian leap, but it is only now, because his faith no longer requires theoretical buttressing, that he is not made uncomfortable by saying so, that he is able to examine from a position of disinterest doctrines once too useful to be endangered by scrutiny, and find them wanting. "The most difficult problem in personal knowledge," he suggests, "whether of oneself or of others, is the problem of guessing when to think as a historian and when to think as an anthropologist" (HC, p. 43). As convert, it was necessary for Auden to think as a historian, to defend the principle of religious commitment by emphasizing our aloneness and the quest for meaning as a personal responsibility. Today he is finding it increasingly profitable to think as an anthropologist.

One important result is an awakened gratitude for what men share in common, such as external nature, whose benefits are accessible to all, and their own "physical nature," about which general statements can be made. Nature in Auden is ordinarily a vehicle of poetic technique, and, as we shall see, this is still the case; but today nature also appears as something visibly and reassuringly "there," as that which remains when human efforts have met with frustration. Nature is persistently evoked as a restorer of perspective, a delight to the senses offering relief from worldly cares:

. . . your ambient peace
In any case is a cure for, ceasing to think
Of a way to get on, we
Learn to simply wander about . . .

("Ischia," N)

For the poet, our response to nature discloses our nearness to grace; it is a measure of the soul's contentment:

Winds make weather; weather
Is what nasty people are

Nasty about and the nice
Show a common joy in observing . . .
("Winds," SA)

The extravagant sweep here of the labels "nasty" and "nice" deliberately sounds the note of whimsy; whatever his regard for nature, there is little in Auden's attitude of what the eighteenth century called "enthusiasm." He admits in "Mountains" (SA) that even the loveliest view would keep him happy for only five minutes, and the above passage supplies through tone a similar check on claims clearly excessive if taken too literally. But "Mountains" also points out that five minutes is "awfully long" for a fallen creature, and what prevails today in Auden's work is the fallen creature's sense of gratitude for the opportunity to enter a world still essentially innocent. Nature may not be holy with God's immanence for Auden as it was for Blake, but it is the Creation and it is worthy of loving attention. Whatever we may think of the course of history, the visible universe impels us to "*Bless what there is for being*" ("Precious Five," N).

As for our physical nature, though he has entitled a volume *Homage to Clio*, his respect for an older mythological personage, Dame Kind, is more affectionate. She is "our Mum," the lady who fitted us out with flesh and bone, appetites, and a physiological rhythm, and he has written in appreciation a rough and slangy eulogy ("Dame Kind," HC), appropriate to a lady who prefers her passion raw and has no use for euphemism, Mother Nature as a sort of Wife of Bath. That we are biological organisms, dependent for survival on processes we cannot control, is for Auden a fact to be reiterated with tender respect. Whether recording his admiration for the steadfast and dependable human bone:

Wherever our personalities go
(And, to tell the truth, we do not know),
The solid structures they leave behind
Are no discredit to our kind,

("An Island Cemetery," HC)

or berating his body in mock chagrin at its embarrassing needs and tastes:

> Really, must you,
> Over-familiar
> Dense companion,
> Be there always?
> The bond between us
> Is chimerical surely:
> Yet I cannot break it—
>
> ("You," AH)

Auden derives an amused satisfaction from acknowledging what Niebuhr refers to as our "creatureliness" and undercutting by this process our more pretentious posturings. "Enthusiasm" is one of these: an admirer of "stars that do not give a damn," he admits that he does not miss them during the day, that were they all to disappear, he would "learn to look at an empty sky/ And feel its total dark sublime" ("The More Loving One," HC). Though some of us prefer to render obeisance to the "hypochondriac/ Blue-Stocking from Provence," Auden finds it "mannerly" to give thanks that we are "corporal contraptions"; whatever our styles, we are indebted for existence to Dame Kind and her years of dirty work.

Behind such poking fun at lofty sentiment and the human sense of self-importance there is discernible in Auden himself a beguiling sanity and a sense of genuine humility. Like the blessed in "In Praise of Limestone," who are without anxiety, Auden no longer seems to care what angle he is regarded from, seems only too willing to expose to general view his penchants and frivolities. One is reminded that a long time ago he declared that the writers he would prefer to be like were Potter, Carroll, and Lear. At the same time, his whimsies are hardly naive; in fact they are wiles. Taking a hint from his suggestion that the fool in *Lear* is really an inspired advisor representing the "sense of reality" rejected by the king, F. W. Cook acutely remarks that Auden himself has been playing the role of "wise fool" *vis a vis* the modern "Managerial State,"[3] trying to bring to light, by means of an insistence upon the personal, the playful, and the eccentric, the unreality of regarding people as statistics. Stephen Spender observes that Auden's "serious insistence on unseriousness—on reducing the cosmos to the personal and gossipy even—sets private experience up in opposition to (a) the public calamity threatening at every moment to destroy us and (b) the managerial view of society."[4] In fact, after narrowing his view in the forties to the existential predicament, Auden has returned to the problem of man in his social context. Initially, in 1940, he had welcomed the atomization of society because by destroying traditional social restrictions, it encouraged individualism. But he also saw that the need for social cohesion would be increasingly implemented by the State, and, in "The Unknown Citizen," he had protested against dehumanizing institutionalism. By 1948, the situation was such that he could declare: "No private citizen to-day thinks seriously, 'Here is superior me and there are all those other people,'" but instead: "Here are we, all in the same boat, and there is It, the Government." Two years later, he suggests that perhaps the duty of the intellectual is to constitute himself member of a sort of Loyal Opposition—"defending, not for his own sake only but for all, the inalienable rights of the individual person against encroachment by an overzealous government."[5]

In this campaign against Caesar, Auden's object of attack is not, of course, government itself, so much as the mentality of government, the tendency of those holding power to think of hu-

[3] "The Wise Fool," *Twentieth Century,* CLXVIII (Sept. 1960), pp. 219-27.

[4] "Seriously Unserious," *Poetry,* LXXVIII (Sept. 1951), p. 352.

[5] See, respectively, "Tradition and Value," *New Republic,* CII (Jan. 1940), p. 90; "Yeats as an Example," *Kenyon Review,* X (Spring 1948), p. 191; *Poets of the English Language,* ed. with Norman Holmes Pearson (New York: Viking Press, 1950), V, Introduction, p. xxv.

man nature as something to be shaped in the interests of efficient living, to be organized for the common good as revealed to bureaucracy, so that the ideal citizen emerges a uniform product of predictable habits, a member of what Kierkegaard called "the Public" and Auden identifies, in "The Chimeras" (N), as a dragon who uses our own strength to destroy us when we make the mistake of believing in its reality. His battle tactics range from the direct assault to snide harassment, from a cutting if unmalicious analysis of managerial types as captives to a role, not even genuine Caesars who can let their hair down in private ("The Managers," N)—to sly thrusts, such as the observation, in "Mountains," that the landscape appeals because "the nearest person who could have me hung is/ Some ridges away." More pervasively, Auden marshals against Caesar's seriousness our impulse towards play and against his plans our innate dislike of regimentation. Opposing those who would condition us for our own good, have us all "somatotyped, baptized, taught baseball" ("Numbers and Faces," N), his efforts as a champion of the "unpolitical," of an "Eden" where gossip is the main source of public information and the form of government is "Absolute monarchy, elected for life by lot" (DH, p. 7), counter the trend to officialism by suggesting the value of the personal and heterodox.

Auden's Christian view of things, like Niebuhr's, identifies sin as either pride or sensuality. Both reflect our fall from faith, our insistence upon setting our own will above the will of God; but if one entails a wish to choose our own necessity, to substitute for the elusive order of creation our own self-justifying system, the other is the self-love frustrating all systems, a perversity deriving from our intractable creatureliness. At times, this element has seemed to Auden a principal adversary, the foe of enlightenment. Today, he takes pleasure in celebrating our creatureliness because he discerns in it, in the natural part of human nature, a formidable ally. The makeshift efforts of secular authority arbitrarily to decree order in a disordered postwar world are symbolized in "Memorial for the City" (N) by the barbed wire; it "neither argues nor explains" and, confusing our sense of what we are, it holds in place Caesar's distorting mirror. Fortunately, behind the mirror, "our Image" is unchanged. It is the old Adam in us, which speaks in the poem as "Our Weakness":

> Had he listened to me Oedipus would never have left
> Corinth; I cast no vote at the trial of Orestes.
> I fell asleep when Diotima spoke of love . . .

For Auden today, our weakness is also our strength. It is the Sancho Panza in us, willing to be led along, after a fashion, by the ambitious plans of Don Quixote, but having too great a regard for the solid pleasures of flesh and belly to be wholly taken in by Utopian schemes, too much respect for the discomforts of exertion to be very efficient in carrying them out.[6] In our indolence and our love of pleasure, our innate distrust of the overly spiritual and abstract, Caesar encounters an unconquerable adversary:

> As for Metropolis, that too-great city; her delusions
> are not mine.
> Her speeches impress me little, her statistics less;
> to all who dwell on the public side of her
> mirrors resentments and no peace.
> At the place of my passion her photographers are
> gathered together; but I shall rise again
> to hear her judged.

As the image suggests, Auden finds in our creatureliness, in the unheroic predilections of a creature of flesh, the savior that will frustrate Caesar and keep up human.

External nature, too, commends itself to his attention as a corrective to pride, for it has no wish "to be stood in/ Rows or at

[6] Cf. Auden's comment that as Sancho Panza, the self, seen by Don Quixote, the ego, the individual never prays: "As Don Quixote seen by Sancho Panza, he never giggles." "Hic et Ille," *Encounter,* VI (April 1956), p. 34.

right angles" ("Ode to Gaea," SA) and the innocent relief it offers from the taxing concerns of an overorganized world suggests the validity of an opposing set of values. In communicating these, Auden's instrument is parable, a form of discourse pursuing a moral import by finding in the familiar phenomenon or occasion an embodied commentary on human affairs, subject to exposition. Parable has always been the principal mode of Auden's literary criticism, and today it is also the dominant mode in his art. Parables of "place," such as "In Praise of Limestone" (N) or "Goodbye to the Mezzogiorno" (HC), perhaps his best, come most readily to mind. His method in each is to find in setting an objective correlative for a style of life, so that the analysis of setting serves as vehicle of a moral lesson. One thinks, too, of "Ischia" or "Airport" (N), "Pleasure Island" (N) or almost any of the "Bucolics" (SA), in all of which a particular variety of landscape, because associated with one or a number of typed responses, becomes a text for the interpretation of human proclivities. Whatever its subject, the object of parable is to exploit the particular for its value as paradigm, as "Airport" will illustrate. In this poem, setting functions primarily as a model "nowhere" in which we do not exist as individuals, to make the point that our humanity is realized only in personal relationship to space and time.

If "Airport" makes use of Caesar's world to discredit his values, Auden's technique more often is to oppose Caesar to nature, the solemn, bureaucratic, and abstract, to the vivid and sensual, the utilitarian to the playful. In "Lakes," he toys with the notion that a lake as a small, circumscribed pivot of affairs acts to encourage the personal life and an intimacy at odds with international friction:

> Sly Foreign Ministers should always meet beside one,
> For, whether they walk widdershins or deasil,
> Its path will yoke their shoulders to one liquid centre.

"Streams," another of the "Bucolics," suggests that by "opposing identical banks/ Transferring the loam from Huppim/ To Muppim and back," water makes fun of our quarrels. In the state of a nation's woods, he finds an index of its faith in a worthwhile future:

> A well-kempt forest begs Our Lady's grace;
> Someone is not disgusted, or at least
> Is laying bets upon the human race
> Retaining enough decency to last . . .
>
> ("Woods," SA)

By the process of parable, the pleasures of nature are not only evoked so as to suggest their intrinsic virtue; functioning paradigmatically, they become symbolic of Arcadian values and place in perspective the activities of a creature too earnestly engrossed in history:

> Not to lose time, not to get caught,
> Not to be left behind, not, please! to resemble
> The beasts who repeat themselves, or a thing like water
> Or stone whose conduct can be predicted, these
> Are our Common Prayer, whose greatest comfort is music
> Which can be made anywhere, is invisible,
> And does not smell.
>
> ("In Praise of Limestone,"N)

Thus the anxiety of a divided being capable of creating history; but a limestone region made for pleasure, or a Mediterranean island like Ischia, furnishes a deflating lesson:

> Noble are the plans of the shirt-sleeved engineer,
> But luck, you say, does more. What design could
> have washed
> With such delicate yellows
> And pinks and greens your fishing ports . . . ?
>
> ("Ischia," N)

A good look around us reminds us that we are created beings, limited in our powers, but with much to be grateful for; it stimulates a healthy sense of humility.

Auden does not suggest, however, as in his early work, where the self is championed at the ego's expense, that our salvation lies in *following* nature, that moral effort is unimportant. In proclaiming our imperfectability, our creatureliness, and our need for play, his purpose is to undermine the invalid and dehumanizing claims of secular authority. A setting such as Ischia provides a salutary perspective on human endeavor precisely because it offers no delusions:

> . . . upon
> Your quays, reminding the happy
> Stranger that all is never well
> Sometimes a donkey breaks out into a choking wail
> Of utter protest at what is the case . . .

We do not forget that there is a time "to salute the conqueror" and attend to the business of history.

This is the task of constructing the Just City, and if Auden fears that the planners and reformers, "Reducing to figures/ What is the matter," will, if left to themselves, create the False City in which no individual will find it possible to be himself, he is also aware that, in intention, they share his goal and are indispensable to its accomplishment. Auden is not a foe to modern technology and its comforts. Not long ago, he ventured to say that though he appreciated his refrigerator at cocktail time, he doubted that he would ever write a panegyric ode to it,[7] but now, celebrating the installation of an American kitchen in Austria ("Grub First, Then Ethics," AH), he has done very nearly that. "Pompous Apollo" clearly has gifts denied to mercurial natures:

[7] "The Dyer's Hand: Poetry and the Poetic Process," *Anchor Review,* No. 2 (1957), p. 290.

If he would leave the self alone,
Apollo's welcome to the throne,
    Fasces and falcons;
He loves to rule, has always done it;
The earth would soon, did Hermes run it,
    Be like the Balkans.

("Under Which Lyre," N)

The trouble with the managers is not their love of efficiency, but their failure to appreciate the uniqueness of individuals, so that they insist on meddling where they have no business. Auden's fear is that "we seem likely to live increasingly in a world of one culture and many faiths," and that in such a world, the "heretic" will be, "not the man who chooses his own truth, but the man who insists on his own taste, who, say, dislikes ice-cream or Italian opera in English."[8] In defense of such heresy, his own efforts are designed to reveal that the Just City will be one in which the basis of public values is a recognition of the priority of personal life.

A glance at a college catalogue[9] under the listings for Anthropology will reveal that it is mainly as an anthropologist that Auden pursues his aim. The following are some headings that strike the attention:

> . . . the anticipation of culture among the animals . . . and culture as an adaptive mechanism . . . Comparison of ways of life . . . Implications of these styles of life for understanding of human behavior in general . . . interpretations of artifacts of man's material culture . . . study of the relation of man and his physical environment, the role of technology in mediating between the two . . . The position of man in the animal kingdom.

[8] "Religion and the Intellectuals," *Partisan Review,* XVII (Feb. 1950), p. 128.

[9] I have used the catalogue nearest to hand, that of Michigan State University.

Auden has always been attracted, of course, to the long view of an anthropological perspective, but today his work displays all of these interests. An observer of human nature as revealed in the evolving development of the species, in "Memorial for the City" he has traced the achievements of the City through history; in poems such as "Sext" (SA) and "Thanksgiving for a Habitat" (AH), he examines the implications of its vocations and its architecture, and in "Good-bye to the Mezzogiorno" of its divergent life-styles. "The Geography of the House" and "Encomium Balnei" (AH) are occupied with the ritual of our daily habits, "Hands" (HC) and "Their Lonely Betters" (N) with the tools of gesture and of language which distinguish us from the animals. His concern for the deities and tutelary spirits that evoke our homage is evident in his portrayal of Clio and Dame Kind. From all of this there emerges a sort of myth of contemporary *anthropos*. Despite the comment that products of the mythopoeic imagination are "instantaneously recognizable by the fact that their existence is not defined by their social and historical context" (DH, p. 407), Auden's own endeavor has been increasingly directed towards establishing such a connection, towards using the resources of mythic figuration, not to resolve existence into universal essence, but to place in perspective the hopes and patterns of our culture and submit them to analysis.

There is, of course, nothing new in this procedure. The typical Auden poem is not a direct rendering of experience but a conceptual construct, in which persons, places, and events are mainly the visible embodiments of perceived relationships, assimilated as subject matter only so far as they can be interpreted by intellect. His use of wit as a means of dissecting the specimen case (many of his more recent poems are really extended witticisms), his predilection for personification, parable, and allegory—each of these reflects the habit of examining things as they signify a general import rather than as they directly engage the senses or the emotions. But more and more the terms of analysis have shifted. The allegorical constructs once typical in his work were such things as Gross Hunger, Justice, and Falsehood, and only recently they were the Garden and the Desert, the Word and the Flesh, and the Way. Now they are Eden and New Jerusalem, *Homo Ludens* and Tum-Tum, Caesar and Dame Kind and the City; and though some of these are carry-overs, there is enough differentiating each group to evidence on the whole not only a progression of roles—the humanitarian social reformer giving way to the convert to theology, who is succeeded by the observer of culture—but the accompanying shift of method with objective. The early terms are mainly convenient notations for familiar conceptions, whereas the later, in use, are active conceptual agents which, by mythologizing the modern situation, render its concerns historically recognizable, and function as instruments of cultural analysis. The antitypes meeting in "Vespers" (SA), examples of the familiar Auden technique of balancing opposites so as to suggest their one-sidedness, will illustrate. Representing contrasting points of view towards the social goal of the good life, Utopian and Arcadian, are also, as a result of the perspective gained by naming them, historical types, who define the cross-currents in our culture because they exemplify the particular form in which the conflict between body and soul, between work and play, arises in contemporary society. In "The Managers," too, an analysis giving mythic status to a modern class is an investigation of historical change—of the present form in which power is exercised.

In keeping with his conviction that history is meaningful, Auden's aim as an observer of culture is to examine our progress towards the Just City. The advantage of the anthropological outlook is that it provides a means of indicating the values according to which we organize our resources and found our customary preferences:

> Nobody I know would like to be buried
> with a silver cocktail shaker,

a transistor radio and a strangled
daily help . . .

("Thanksgiving for a Habitat," AH)

The first things to strike us about this passage are its whimsy of suggestion and its command of topical detail, but after a moment its point registers. A glance at ancient custom discloses the egalitarian temper of the present day—our remoteness from a time when possessions were a privilege of the strong and could be conceived as personal.

A cognizance of culture also alerts us to the lure of the fashionable. In Popean couplets themselves making the point, Auden observes that "Each age has its own mode of listening":

We know the *Mozart* of our fathers' time
Was gay, rococo, sweet, but not sublime,
A Viennese Italian; that is changed
Since music critics learned to feel "estranged";
Now it's the Germans he is classed amongst,
A *Geist* whose music was composed from *Angst* . . .

("Metalogue to the Magic Flute," HC)

This mildly ironic view of existential solemnity was perhaps already a part of Auden when he wrote *The Age of Anxiety*, but now his perspective and his manner match. The distance from which he regards our humble struggles expresses, not disdain, but a recognition of human fallibility and an acceptance of limitations. Underlying the anthropologist's observations there is a tolerant and engaging humility, anchored in religious foundations. For Auden is aware that "The Holy Ghost/ does not abhor a golfer's jargon" ("Whitsunday in Kirchstetten," AH), that it is in culture that individuals find the patterns of self-expression. A confrontation with the boisterous mores of the Mezzogiorno ("Good-bye to the Mezzogiorno," HC) may be an instructive experience for children of a northern "guilt culture," but it also reveals that between those for whom life is a "*Bildungsroman* and those to whom living/ Means to-be-visible-now," the gulf is unbridgeable. Pointing the differences between court poets dependent "for bread on the moods of a/ Baroque Prince" and the contemporary, more privileged variety, between the "Rational City" envisioned by the French Revolution and the "Conscious City" created by later, tortured explorers of self, or drawing attention, less momentously, to the distance between "Chaste Milady" and a modern mom, Auden finds in the analysis of culture a means to make us known to ourselves, aware of our defects and values and thankful for our prerogatives.

The awareness and gratitude are particularly evident when culture is seen as a reflection of man's unique ability, despite his creatureliness, to determine his mode of life and build a world. After all, another function of the anthropological outlook is to throw into relief the peculiar make-up of the species, so as to remind us of our capacities and of the factors which impose limitations upon our will, of our peculiarly ambiguous position in the Great Chain of Being. Auden points out that though there are masons and carpenters among the beasts, there are no architects, that, gifted with self-consciousness, only human beings know the meaning of "If" ("The Birth of Architecture," AH). This sort of distinction, with its reference to the difference between nature and history, is now a staple and engaging feature of his work. Formerly examined to analyze the riddle of existence, the relationship between nature and history, now that Auden has found his solution in Christian faith, provides the background of reference structuring his represented view of things. As already indicated, one result is an undercutting of human pretensions. Like it or not, we have needs and pleasures that are controlled by Dame Kind. As devoted lover, Auden admits that "Thousands have lived without love, not one without water" ("First Things First," HC). Whimsically, he shows us a bard interrupting his elevated labors to postpone "his dying with a dish/ Of several suffocated fish"

("Hunting Season," SA). The point of these observations is that as a creature, man, just like the other creatures, participates in nature, where he is capable only of "behavior," not of deed, his life as an individual indistinguishable from that of the species; and Auden is fond of making this point; he remarks that "the subject of the verb/ to-hunger is never a name" ("Grub First, Then Ethics," AH), that the act of kind is not our own but Aphrodite's deed ("Dichtung und Wahrheit," HC). Nature is the realm of the determined and habitual—of birth, copulation, and death, pleasure and pain, sensation without reflection; and the poet reminds us that much of our living takes place on this plane of being, that like the creatures who know no words "We, too, make noises when we laugh or weep" ("Their Lonely Betters," N), that we become at any drink or meal an "animal of taste," that a significant part of our existence is patterned in cycles by the "revolving wheel/ Of appetite and season" ("Precious Five," N). In "Memorial for the City" (N), this view of things is expressed through the eyes of the crow and the camera: impressed by physical presence, they "magnify earth"; they record not unique actions but—"the way things happen"; by composing a moment into an "eternal fact," they suggest that things could not have been otherwise.

This view of existence is false, of course, or, at best, an outsider's view, only partly true. The greater part of Auden's effort is designed to complete the picture, to remind us that we are capable of history as well as of creaturely behavior, that the power of self-consciousness grants us not only the capacity to shape our lives, but to find meaning in our experience. Just as he is aware of our involvement in nature, Auden is habitually alert to the distinctions separating us from the rest of creation, to the hierarchy implied by the Chain of Being. To observe one's surroundings is to survey the ranks of creation. With a depth of implication, he points out that "cenobite, mosses and lichen" are "sworn to/ Station and reticence" ("Hammerfest," AH), that though pack-hunters dine *en famille,* only man, "superogatory beast," can "do the honors of a feast" ("Tonight at Seven-Thirty," AH). By the parable technique already discussed, anything that is a part of culture and distinguishes us from the creatures becomes paradigmatic of what it means to be human. What it means to be human, and to be a person, is now the principal focus of Auden's interests. That we have Proper names evidences the fact that, unlike the robins, who sing only the "Robin-Anthem," we are free to express ourselves as unique individuals. However, a name may also stand, as in "A Change of Air" (AH), for the customary role by which the self defines itself, and from which it must sometimes relieve itself by seeking anonymity. Language, too, is a mark of our freedom, of our power to assume "responsibility for time." As "A Short Ode to a Philologist" (AH) points out, "free/ Speech is a tautology." Architecture, too, since our dwellings represent "someone's idea of the body/ that should have been his" ("Thanksgiving for a Habitat" AH), is emblematic; like every creation of culture, it testifies to our ability to envision things otherwise and bring novelty into existence. Considering whatever we do as significant of an interplay between nature and history, of our confinement within the former sphere or of our emergence into the latter, Auden finds a rich source of parable in the seemingly inconsequential:

> In a brothel, both
> The ladies and gentlemen
> Have nicknames only.
>
> (Postscript, "The Cave of Making," AH)

The truth is that, though intent upon honoring our creatureliness and wary of pride, Auden now celebrates the human release from the rule of nature, so long associated with the Fall, as a *felix culpa.* Though once he envied a duck's indifference, he now considers our mindless brethren and concludes that we have reason to be thankful:

Woken at sunup to hear
A cock pronouncing himself himself
Though all his sons had been castrated and eaten,
I was glad I could be unhappy . . .

("Homage to Clio," HC)

The "Horae Canonicae" sequence (SA) reminds us that freedom entails a severance from the obligatory operation of "law," and that, as a consequence, sin is present in every act by which we express self-will. As a result, the performance of our social tasks brings a daily, symbolic re-enactment of the crucifixion, a rejection of the Word made flesh as a human community in which word and flesh are mutually fulfilling. Artist and reformer are reciprocally guilty in this, the one tending to forget that we are equal as creatures and have material needs, the other that we differ as spiritual beings and must follow our tastes. But their sacrificial victim Auden portrays as our own human innocence. And he acknowledges himself grateful for the ability to put vocation before appetite, to establish the values on which authority rests, even for the capacity to form a "crowd" (something possible only for beings with a personal identity to surrender). These things enable sin, but they are also the means by which we enter into history, and they make possible our adventure towards the Just City.

As distinct from nature, history is created in the free acts by which we give significance to time, and its ruling imperative, "To thine own self, be true," may be contrasted with the goal of the creatures, whose development is a given: "To thyself, be enough."[10] The observer of history runs into difficulty, however, as Auden suggests in picturing the muse of history as unspeaking

[10] "To be enough to oneself means to have no conscious ego standing over against the self, to be unable to say no to oneself, or to distinguish fantasy from reality, not to be able to lie, to have no name and answer to Hi or to any loud cry." *The Enchafèd Flood* (London: Faber and Faber, 1951), p. 78.

and unrecognizable ("Homage to Clio"), the difficulty of distinguishing between historical event and its personal content:

> From gallery-grave and the hunt of a wren-king
> to Low Mass and trailer camp
> is hardly a tick by the carbon clock, but I
> don't count that way nor do you . . .
> ("The Birth of Architecture," AH)

For creatures cognizant of time, the existential quality of experience is unique; it is the "once-for-all that is not seen nor said" ("One Circumlocution," N) and accounting for the fact that "love, or truth in any serious sense,/ Like orthodoxy, is a reticence" (" 'The Truest Poetry is the Most Feigning,' " HC). In the serious sense regardful of their bearing on the reality of our lives, Auden has been increasingly concerned with the meaning of such things as love and truth and, not least of all, orthodoxy. But he has found that as a result of the depersonalization increasingly attendant upon the carrying out of our social functions, the "Public Realm" is no longer in our time the sphere of "revelatory personal deeds" (DH, p. 80). As individuals participating in the roles, institutions, and customs of our culture, we differentiate the human being from the creature. In our language and dress, our means of entertainment and of livelihood, human nature finds its historical form of expression. In the "Public Realm," however, we are apt to function as members of a "Public," for today it is primarily the "Private Realm" in which we reveal ourselves *as persons*. Auden's problem, of course, is that to the poet as anthropologist this is, or would seem, a field closed to observation, and it is this in the existential sense. But once again he has found a solution in parable; the artifacts and amenities making up civilization and distinguishing us from the creatures furnish commentary not only on the relationship of historical beings to nature but on that of unique selves to the culture determining the circumstances in which selfhood is disclosed.

Particularly is his most recent volume, *About the House*, with the privileges of the City reflected in the comforts of his own home, he has been able to suggest the experience of unique "I's" by showing that it is mainly among the "furniture" and in the informal rituals of private life that we reveal our essential selves and enter into "thou-thou" relationships with others. Without ceasing to be an observer of the visible and familiar, he has been able to bear witness to the reticencies of personal life, to disclose in the constitution of the household and in domestic routine the values of this life set forth in parable. His treatment of the bathroom will illustrate. There is significance in the fact that a bathroom has only an inside lock and wholly belongs to its occupant:

> among us
> to withdraw from the tribe at will
> be neither Parent
> Spouse nor Guest
> is a sacrosanct
> political right
>
> ("Encomium Balnei")

In accord with this observation, the daily bath is offered to our attention as the occasion of a health-giving release from roles and suggests the value of such privileged moments when a sage can "be silly without shame/ present a Lieder Abend/ to a captive audience of his toes." The other rooms of the house are equally fertile as fields for observation; in the living-room, one can read the signs of a "secular faith," and in this technique of reading from the character of our surroundings and habitual preferences a statement of what and who we are, Auden has become adept. Even staircases have symbolic significance; they indicate the many selves which compose us and the necessity of distinguishing among them. Doors are not "emphatic enough" to mark the transition of going to bed:

The switch from personage,
with a state number, a first and family name,
to the naked Adam or Eve, and vice versa,
should not be off-hand or abrupt: a stair retards it
to a solemn procession.

("The Cave of Nakedness")

It would be easy to multiply examples of this sort of parable of the commonplace, but the fact is Auden now instinctively views things in terms of their parabolic significance, and almost any passage selected at random would serve. In the forties, he had employed parable as an extension into art of his practice of literary interpretation—in relation to *The Tempest* in "The Sea and the Mirror" and to the Nativity story in "For the Time Being." But now, as Richard Ohmann has observed,[11] his allegorical text is the real world, the one we have created and which expresses our unique constitution, as well as the "Immortal Commonwealth/ which is there regardless." In the exercise of the anthropologist's perspective, he has arrived at a means of structuring his observations which ensures them a burden of implication and a paradigmatic import however humble their reference.

Yet it would be misleading to picture him as a purely detached observer, preaching moral lessons in an indirect and, therefore, inoffensive form. The values he expounds are his own, and they are effectively conveyed because they are set forth with a balanced awareness and a perspective on self-importance which acknowledges their genuine personal meaning. Auden frequently talks about himself today, and with a candor quite disarming; witness his "Thanksgiving for a Habitat" (AH):

what I dared not hope or fight for
is, in my fifties, mine, a toft-and-croft

11 "Auden's Sacred Awe," in *Auden: A Collection of Critical Essays*, ed. Monroe K. Spears (Englewood Cliffs, N.J.: Prentice-Hall, 1964), p. 178.

where I needn't, ever, be at home *to*
those I am not at home *with* . . .

There is cleverness here and a cultivated archness, but few can fail to see that they are meant to rescue a modest delight from sentimentality. It is characteristic that the impulse towards self-satisfaction is quickly checked—by a sober awareness of what privacy is for and a humble sense of gratitude:

. . . not a cradle,
a magic Eden without clocks,
and not a windowless grave, but a place
I may go both in and out of.

As in the above, almost everything Auden writes today suggests elusively a quality of inwardness in his response to the things of this world shaped by the conviction that life is a blessing. Paradoxically, it is a quality most strongly felt where it would be least anticipated, in turns of phrase approaching the precious, in chattiness, and in whimsy; and it is no more susceptible of demonstration than was Kierkegaard's perception of a comparable quality in Lessing. But perhaps, when closest to direct expression, it may be known by its want of pretense, its simple acceptance of the things which constitute us, as in Auden's memoriam to Louis MacNeice:

. . . I wish you hadn't
caught that cold, but the dead we miss are easier
to talk to: with those no longer
tensed by problems one cannot feel shy and, anyway,
when playing cards or drinking
or pulling faces are out of the question, what else is there
to do but talk to the voices
of conscience they have become?

("The Cave of Making," AH)

"Tonight at Seven-Thirty" (AH), a treatment of the dinner party as a ceremonial feast, prescribes the kind of guests required, the proper size of the gathering, and the manners which must prevail for this "worldly rite" to retain its efficacy. The poem is a parable on the meaning of "authentic comity" in a world where public occasions no longer foster this experience. But we do not lose sight of the fact that what is valued here is of personal appeal, that the appreciation conveyed for dapatical fare and human relationship is Auden's appreciation, and that it betokens, not the connoisseur's fastidiousness, but the created being's right regard for "Nature's bounty" and what "grace of Spirit" can provide.

On all of this, of course, the influence of Auden's Christianity is incalculably great. He has written that poetry is essentially an affirmation of being, and this conviction now informs his work as it could not be said to at a time when religious themes were more conspicuous upon the surface. Auden seems at ease with himself today, able to accept imponderables in a spirit of humility, to be thankful and patient, yet, like the kind of dinner guest he approves of, without kidding himself that our care is consolable or falling into complacency. Despite the mock ferocity he sometimes invokes to defend the privileged domain of his privacy ("I have no gun, but I can spit."), those poems touching most directly on the particulars of a Christian existence are notable for the modesty of aim revealed, for their appreciation of the hindrances which stand against the attainment of even the small virtues of personal life. Reminiscent of the *Screwtape Letters,* he pictures the little provocations that tempt us to betray our better selves as the creation of minor devils: Tubervillus, "demon of gossip and spite" ("Cattivo Tempo," N), "Merax & Mullin" (HC), philological fiends. He can be trivial today, and he refuses to be solemn and polished, but these traits mark his aversion for "imps of mawk and hooey," his awareness that human emotions are a mixture "Half humbug and half true." One recognizes in the contrivances of his art—in his fanciful personifications and quirkish diction, or in the way many of his poems seem to accumulate by spurts and arbitrary shifts of direction—a way of signalling his readers that art is play and only a feigned image of things, that speech is a privilege belying the ineffable.

Despite the occasional references to last stands in the passes, the mood of crisis once so prevalent is no longer an Auden characteristic. Nature and history are now categories of observation serving an affirmation of personal being; he is no longer examining the conflict between ego and self so as to justify existence. In one sense, Auden's quest has come to a conclusion along "A Permanent Way," for he has reached and now instinctively reflects as an attitude Simeon's recognition that "our redemption is no longer a question of pursuit but of surrender to Him who is always and everywhere present." On the other hand, he observes that "Christianity is a way, not a state, and a Christian is never something one is, only something one can pray to become."[12] This effort, though subtly so, is a distinctive aspect of his work, so that we may continue to expect from him, although now more by force of example and indirect suggestion than by precept, guidance on the question of how we are to live and to love.

Though always informed by the awareness that we are social beings whose personal interest requires a concern for the Just City, Auden's quest has been an effort to discover the secret of authentic life. If in the thirties his views underwent considerable change and were sometimes expressed with an irritating dogmatism suggesting abrupt and arbitrary reversals of outlook rather than coherent development, it is clear in retrospect that his conversion to Christianity climaxed a movement of thought heading in a single direction and that a constant underlying factor accompanying this movement, and the development subsequent to his conversion, has been the rejection of dualism and a vindication of the body. It should be understood, though, that it is only in the very early work, if at all, that this principle stands unqualified as

[12] Foreword to Emile Cammaerts, *The Flower of Grass* (New York: Harper & Brothers, 1945), p. xvi.

a plea for the uninhibited life. The volitional ego has two wishes, Auden writes: "On the one hand it wishes to be free of all demands made upon it by the self or the conscience or the outer world . . . On the other hand, it wishes to be important, to find its existence meaningful, to have a *telos* . . ." (DH, p. 113). The movement of thought lasting throughout the 1930's presupposes that our *telos* exists in natural law and, at the start, it finds in the ego's warped exercise of freedom a principal source of frustration. But it is a movement charting its course from the recognition that in a sick society unconscious impulses are no longer governed by natural law, and its direction is *away* from the notion that existence is meaningful to the degree that energies are immediately gratified and towards an ever-greater acceptance of the ego's role as an agent of order. In 1940, this movement reaches a point of re-definition. Auden now affirms his faith that the ego finds its *telos* not in nature but in the will of God, which is to say, in Christian revelation, which directs that "we are required to love/ All homeless objects that require a world" ("Canzone"). It is in relation to this obligation that our freedom is meaningful, and the result is that Auden now finds many of our secular activities "unserious." But this is not to be construed as a weakening of his opposition to dualism. Far from condoning an attitude of passive withdrawal, he insists as a Christian that the Flesh is redeemed by the Word, that the human Eros is actualized only in particular acts in time. With reference to his poetry of social action, he has recently commented that he and his colleagues of the thirties "made a great mistake in writing about things we really did not know enough about," but he adds that he does not think their views were wrong.[13] The Just City may be beyond human effort, but human effort is obliged to approximate to it.

Although the Christian view of evil as a product of the fallen will was perhaps the decisive intellectual factor in Auden's con-

[13] "'Difficult' Poetry?" *The Listener,* LXIII (May 1960), p. 788.

version, it is not difficult to see why this notion was long resisted. If one regards the basic energy of existence as love, evil seems an anomaly, something that should not be there to begin with; for this reason Auden's thinking, during a good part of the thirties, was dominated by the idea of health, the state in which one is obedient to natural law, with evil regarded as illness, an abnormality. Illness at its most severe takes the form of a death wish, the self-destructive response to their inner energies of those taught by a repressive morality to fear their energies, so that in defiance of their best interests they cling to the established and familiar. Love is simply healthy, uninhibited life in vital relation to Eros —a condition gained when one has swept the insensitive refuse from the burning core.

Auden's criticism defines the hero, rather noncommittally, as the "exceptional individual," but more specific conceptions, emerging at different times, furnish insight into his changing assumptions. It is significant that in Auden's early work the man of action, especially when conceived as a leader figure, is much in evidence. However, he is also suspect since his exploits may represent neurotic efforts at compensation. The hero is the "Truly Strong Man," who is pure in heart and thus healthy: "He was essentially free and easy . . . without worries or inhibitions . . . He was entirely without fear; therefore he could never catch an infectious disease. And without guilt: therefore he was immune from syphilis."[14] Not only an ideal, the Truly Strong man is also, to an extent, a model for direct emulation, for he evidences the health of inner desires, supporting the hope in cure "without confession of the ill." This hope is treated ironically at many points, as the delusion of the wounded, but the point does not become decisive for Auden until the destructiveness of emergent fascism offers proof that desire itself, in sick individuals, is poisoned. He is then forced to insist on the difference between the pristine impulses of the Im-

[14] Christopher Isherwood, *Lions and Shadows* (Norfolk: New Directions, 1947), p. 304.

personal Unconscious and the immature and dangerous urges resulting from repression and from the formation of a *personal* unconscious mirroring the anxieties and prohibitions of society. Evil continues to appear as illness; Auden's attention simply shifts to the social system which promotes and is sustained by illness, so that cure is revealed to be dependent upon the defeat of this system.

Accordingly, the hero becomes, like the Airman after his sudden awakening, the man conscious of his enemies, whether interior or external, and determined to take rational action to secure their downfall. He is the person armed with understanding against the possibility that his desires may reflect immature fixations, that his usual thinking, in both Freudian and Marxist spheres of reference, may be "interested" thinking. It is at this time that Auden explains that the hero of the fairy tale succeeds where his older brothers fail, "because confronted with a problem he overcomes it by understanding rather than with force." He continues to regard the claims of the (Impersonal) unconscious as unconditional, to see its shaping of a new social order as inevitable, but he now equates love with social responsibility and personal asceticism rather than with self-gratification. For the moment, love cannot take "that route which is straightest"; the service of love belongs to the enlightened ego and its commitment to the task of enacting conditions favorable to the return of health.

The health ideal is relinquished only with the growth of fascism as a totalitarian menace. By focussing the choice between health, or a crude facsimile of it, and individual responsibility, fascism's effect upon Auden is to clarify the priority in his own mind of freedom and the traditional liberal values—to force the recognition that man's freedom distinguishes him from the creatures. This recognition is reflected in his repudiation of evolutionary necessity—to us Eros is the Yes-man, the bar companion—and in the distinction now established between nature and history. He decides that though the Unconscious "knows it wants something," it "cannot tell what it is until the right something is put into its hands." For this reason, the ego must *choose* to evolve, must *wrestle* with the self, so that out of the interplay between freedom and necessity there may issue, not unreflective well-being, but a clearer definition of the "Truly Human." Auden's heroes are now actual individuals, the great figures of the past who have enriched our understanding and our humanity, who have helped us, indeed, to evolve. They resemble his description of the heroes of "Ethics," who know the True and therefore will the Good, for at this point Auden, like Herod, is a liberal, for whom evil indicates deficient knowledge, particularly of the self. The suspicion that its roots lie deeper, in innate self-love, has yet to undermine his humanism. But the parallel with the heroes of Ethics is defective. On what basis, in light of the findings of contemporary anthropology and sociology, could liberal principles be regarded as universal truths and humanitarian love an unconditional obligation? What Necessary guided "the human effort to make its own fortune"? The war showed that the values of liberalism were not self-supporting, while personal experience, to become "the prey of demonic powers," offered proof that to know the good was not necessarily to will it. Auden's conclusion was that the Fall was complete, that no natural law exists to be obeyed in the wrestling bout between ego and self. This process, though it must test our values, cannot provide them for us:

> The futility of trying to combine both wishes into one, of trying, that is, to have a *telos,* but to find it within oneself not without, is expressed in the myth of Narcissus. Narcissus falls in love with his reflection; he wishes to become its servant, but instead his reflection insists upon being his slave.
>
> (DH, p. 115)

The only thing unconditional about the values of liberalism lay in the Christian revelation from which they derived.

In accepting Christianity, Auden also accepts the problem of evil as indigenous to our fallen state. So long as the Unconditional was thought of as a creation of Eros, it was necessary to locate the source of evil in a factor in some sense extrinsic to our nature, to find its origins in abnormality (illness) or in incompleteness (deficient knowledge). With the Unconditional identified as God's will, our nature itself is revealed to be fallen. The source of evil is our innate self-love, manifesting itself as sin in all those acts, whether of pride or sensuality, which disclose our lack of faith in God. The love to which we are enjoined reveals our dependence upon God; it is *agape,* as defined in the commandment that we are to love our neighbors as ourselves. Auden now accepts the Niebuhrian view that the doctrine of perfection before the Fall refers to the illusion of perfection in the moment of self-transcendence before the act. The Fall refers not to the advent of self-consciousness, but to the subversion of self-consciousness by sin; "original sin" is the bias in our nature causing us to retreat from the anxiety of our divided condition, the temptation to sin, into either sensuality or its opposite, pride, the denial of contingency and creaturely limitation.

As the early hero was the Truly Strong man who was without fear, the hero of Auden's Christian period is the individual without anxiety. Modifying his former interpretation, Auden now suggests that the fairy-tale hero succeeds not through understanding, or even personal merit, but through the assistance of Divine Grace: "His contribution is, firstly, a humility which admits that he cannot succeed without Grace; secondly, a faith which believes that Grace will help him."[15] Thus, he is Kierkegaard's Knight of Faith or he is the prototypical Religious Hero Don Quixote, "self-forgetful" not because he is strong but because he finds his *telos* in a vocation he is committed to with a faith that to ordinary individuals seems madness. In his early days, Auden characterized the cured individual as one in whom the unconscious and the conscious were at one, and it is with this continuing ideal in mind that

[15] "In Praise of the Brothers Grimm," *New York Times Book Review,* Nov. 12, 1944, p. 28.

he asserts that before the fall the volitional ego's two incompatible wishes, to be free and to have a *telos,* were "dialectically related." This is the case with the Religious Hero; having achieved "a passionate obedience in time" ("Mundus et Infans"), he has solved the conflict of divided consciousness; love for him is the fulfilling of the law.

Theoretically, the Christian view, in its emphasis on the individual, cancels the distinction between the exceptional and the average. The Religious Hero is not the man of special gifts but the man of faith, and once we are reflective we are all exceptional, faced with the obligation to become ourselves. Yet this view, which places social considerations in a subordinate position, also provides the basis for a criticism of society; and in such criticism, practical distinctions between the exceptional and the average are unavoidable. It may be observed that on two occasions such distinctions have led Auden towards at least the consideration of an authoritarian viewpoint. Once, in 1947, without coming to any conclusions, he showed himself willing to entertain the proposition that "virtue is prior to liberty, *i.e.,* what matters most is that people should think and act rightly," so that if they cannot they must be made to. Again in 1949 he announced that he would be in favor of censoring Pound's *Pisan Cantos* if he thought it likely (as he did not) that they would be read by people unashamed of their anti-semitic feelings so that in this matter they should be "regarded as children."[16] In light of the suggestion that in *The Age of Anxiety* one may discern Auden's own personal choice already consolidated, the timing of these statements is noteworthy.

But the viewpoint they express has not proved typical. Whatever his attitude might be towards a dictatorship of the just, Auden has been much more concerned with the impediments to a meaningful life furnished by our actual prospects, which he sees as

[16] See, respectively, "Henry James's 'The American Scene,'" *Horizon,* XV (Feb. 1947), pp. 77-90, and "The Question of the Pound Award," *Partisan Review,* XVI (May 1949), pp. 512-13.

living "increasingly in a world of one culture and many faiths." To the exceptional, one element in this situation is a blessing:

> . . . there has never been an age which offered more to the exceptional and less to the average. No longer hampered by a rigid social structure, his intellect no longer limited by traditional or provincial horizons, the gifted and the strong-willed have greater opportunities for good and evil than ever before . . . for when one has great gifts, what answer to the meaning of existence should one require beyond the right to exercise them?[17]

But if the dissolution of traditions has allowed the exceptional to discover in talent a *telos,* it has been of small value to the average who, in the position of Dostoevsky's Underground Man, are offered more and more freedom when "it is precisely freedom in the sense of lack of necessity that is his trouble."[18] In response to this predicament, we now witness increasing activity on all fronts by a benevolently-intentioned but overzealous State, subtle pressure towards the fostering of a vast Kierkegaardian "Public," and the trend towards cultural uniformity whose effect is to make whatever is exceptional, even in private life, suspect.

Artfully, by implication and indirect suggestion, as well as more obvious strategies, Auden has opposed these developments. From the foundation of a Christian faith sanctioning free development of the individual personality, he has defended our right to play, waging a campaign of loyal opposition against the dehumanizing tendencies of the managerial point of view and setting against this point of view the values of authentic personal life. The suggestion that he is now writing the most distinctive and, in many ways, the most distinguished poetry of his career will perhaps come as a surprise, and it would be premature to argue the point since he is still a producing poet from whom we may continue to expect new departures. But, clearly, the motive of his art will no

[17] Foreword to *The Flower of Grass,* pp. xiii-xiv.
[18] *Poets of the English Language,* V, Introduction, p. xxi.

longer be Quest. In orthodoxy Auden has been able to find himself, and his recent work displays a serenity and a quality of inner resourcefulness unmatched before. Without kidding himself that our care is consolable, he now celebrates the virtues of our singular state; though his art remains slyly and subtly instructive, it is no longer intent upon justifying creation. Those who fare well on the Quest find, it would seem, that existence is its own justification, and their reward is an appreciation of the joy and privilege of being alive.

Index

Poems originally untitled are listed by first lines; the title devised for *Collected Poetry* (1945) follows in parentheses.